CHICAGO'S FORGOTTEN TRAGEDY

BILL COSGROVE

authorHOUSE®

AuthorHouse™
1663 Liberty Drive
Bloomington, IN 47403
www.authorhouse.com
Phone: 1-800-839-8640

First published by AuthorHouse 9/17/2010

ISBN: 978-1-4520-7940-0 (e)
ISBN: 978-1-4520-7939-4 (sc)
ISBN: 978-1-4520-7938-7 (hc)

Library of Congress Control Number: 2010913652

Printed in the United States of America

Dedication
This book is dedicated to the memory of my Brother

Michael F. Cosgrove

ACKNOWLEDGMENTS

In the years of gathering all the material for this book, I have had the invaluable assistance of many people.

I would not have been able to write this book without the assistance and encouragement of my late Brother, Michael F. Cosgrove. Mike was the retired Director of Media Affairs of the Chicago Fire Department. He had the vision to see through the flames and smoke, to see the greed of a banker who almost took the funds away from the Widows and Children of the fallen twenty one fireman of the Stockyards fire of 1910.

Thank you, to a guy that I could work with on any project, at any time, William (Bill) Przybylski, He is not a Chicago Fireman, but worked very hard helping raise funds to build the Chicago Firefighters Monument that stands in the entrance of the Chicago Stockyards where 21 firemen were killed on December 22, 1910. He helped make this monument a reality. He encouraged me over and over again to write this book.

I also would not have been able to write this book without the use of reference materials, in particular, <u>Chicago Fire Houses: Volumes I and II</u>. These books let me verify the accuracy of dates, locations, maps, photographs and fire houses

My many thanks also to both Ken Little and Father John McNalis; truly the historians of the Chicago Fire Department.

To my daughter Tracy Ann, who spent countless hours trying to read, and decipher my many pages of hand writing, as she typed the pages of the this book. I thank her for staying up until all hours of the night after she came home from working all day.

To my long time friend and fellow firefighter, Phil Lamm, who had the patience to listen to my ideas, as we looked through many photographs for the book.

To my good friend and a partner, retired firefighter, of Alsip, Illinois, Gene Furmanek, owner of G & L Gifts, who helped me raise funds for the Firemen's Monument. He sold many of my books, and has encouraged me to write this story of the Stockyard fire of 1910.

In February of 2000, I began a partnership with a fireman, to build a monument to honor the fallen twenty-one firemen who were killed in the Stockyards Fire of 1910 and all Chicago firefighters who have died in the line of duty. Through some very difficult times this partner, Bill Cattorini, and I built the monument and a long lasting friendship. Bill Cattorini has helped and supported me throughout the many years of writing this book.

For many years William Alletto was my boss, my chief, and my mentor. Whenever I was unsure about the next part of this book, he would always be there to encourage me to continue. He would always write me little notes of how great he thought the book was going. At any time a question needed to be answered about the Chicago Fire Department, I was always able to call upon him. If it wasn't for him this book would have some misspelled words and some improper grammar. I say thank you to my very good friend, William C. Alletto, retired Deputy Fire Commissioner of the Chicago Fire Department

I would like to acknowledge Irving E. Stieglitz the gentleman that not only took the amazing photographs of the fire in the stockyards, but preserved them for one hundred years. Also to Joseph Smith a gentleman who supplied me with the song by H.E. Davey and H.W. Higgins "The Heroes of The Stockyard Fire".

To my lovely wife, Suzi, who said when I staring writing this book, "Oh, no, not another fire book!" As always, she offered her special talents to edit the manuscript. She did it in a way, at least in my eyes, that made this book a much better read than I ever thought possible. A wife, a Mother, and a Grandmother, that I could not do without; she completes me!

Thank you to my six children who had to listen to the many fire house stories throughout the years, and the support of my books. I apologize for the many birthday parties, Christmas, Thanksgiving and Easters holidays that I missed over the years because of the firehouse.

Like my other three books, contributions will be made to:
The Fireman's Annuity and Benefit Fund of Chicago, The Ende Menzer Walsh Retiree's Widow's and Children's Assistance Fund

Most of the events in this story are true and actual accounts as they occurred. Some of the details and chronology have been altered to preserve anonymity. Some of the names have been changed to protect the confidentiality of the innocent and the guilty. I have been granted a privilege, not through any special inspiration or insight, but through my everyday work.

I am a
"Firefighter"

THE ENEMY

I am more powerful than the combined armies of the world. I have destroyed more men, women and children than all the wars of all nations. I massacre thousands of people every year. I am more deadly than bullets, and I have wrecked more homes than the mightiest guns.

In the United States alone, I steal over 500 million dollars each year. I spare no one and I find my victims among the rich and poor alike, the young and the old, and the strong and the weak. Widows know me to their everlasting sorrow. I loom up in such proportions that I cast my shadow over every field of labor.

I lurk in unseen places and do most of my work silently. You are warned against me, yet you heed me not. I am relentless, merciless and cruel. I am everywhere, in the homes, in the schools, in the factory, on land, in the air, and on th sea.

I bring sickness, degradation and death, yet few seek me out to destroy me. I crush, I maim, I devastate – I will give you nothing and rob you of all you have.

I am your worst enemy – I am rampant fire.

INTRODUCTION

The third watch at Engine Company 59 had just begun. One man stands a watch every two hours throughout the night to be ready to receive a fire call. Bill Weber is the driver of the engine, and he starts his watch by stoking up the fires in the two cast iron wood burning stoves located on the apparatus floor.

Even though the fire house felt warm, young Bill Weber could feel the cold air oozing through the front doors. It was Thursday December 22, 1910. The first day of winter begins today, he thought to himself, as he continued his duties, and it's usually very cold in Chicago. After signing his name, and the time he started his watch into the company journal, he made his way to the stables in the rear of the firehouse to check on the horses. Weber had grown very fond of the horses, because he was the driver who hitched them to the engine, and gave them the commands in the street.

Simultaneously, while Bill Weber was tending to his duties in the firehouse, the night watchman, Paul Leska, of the Nelson-Morris Meat Packing Company was making his rounds checking the exterior of the plant. All of a sudden he discovered heavy black smoke emanating from Beef Plant 7, located at 44th Street and Loomis Avenue in the Chicago Stockyards. Mr. Leska immediately ran toward the burning building and discovered that fire was issuing up a stairway from the basement. At this time, he ran to the adjoining building and pulled the A.D.T. fire alarm. Instantly the alarm was transmitted to the city fire department's fire houses within the Stock Yards at 4:09 am.

While checking the stable, the alarm box in the front of the fire house began to ring. Bill Weber, without any hesitation, began to run to the front, all the time listening and counting the number of bells. Box 2162 was being received, that's our box he thought, as the second round of bells began to

1

ring 2-1-6-2. He looked up at the address board, and at the same time pressed firmly on the red button, and all the bells in the fire house began to ring. The adrenaline began to flow in all the firefighters who began sliding the brass fire pole to the ground floor. Within two minutes the horses were hitched to the engine, and they were out the door.

Upon their arrival at the scene of the fire, there was heavy smoke belching from the loading dock area next to the Beef Plant 7. The hose cart got up close to the dock, and the firefighters began stretching the fire hose in toward the structure. All they knew at this time was that they would need a lot of hose to make it to 43rd Street to the fire hydrant. The 11th Battalion Chief, Martin Lacey, arrived on the scene, and one of the first things he said was, "is there any other way to attack this fire"? "No, Chief", yelled Captain Lannon of Engine Company 50. "We have to get back to the sliding freight doors that lead into the warehouse".

Soon after, Assistant Fire Marshal William Burroughs arrived on the scene. Immediately he put in a second alarm. As a seasoned veteran, with some very hard earned knowledge of fires within the Chicago Stockyards, this Chief did not waste any time. First he sized up the situation, with water at a great distance and freezing temperatures, he requested a third alarm. This one way in platform was a very dangerous manner in which to attack this fire. However, this building did not have any other way to get to the actual seat of the fire. The platform was actually a loading dock, with an old wooden canopy overhead. With a seven story brick building on one side, and a line of railroad boxcars that butted up to the loading dock, the canopy above it formed a tunnel-like effect. Arriving engines were stretching hose lines down the railroad tracks and then under the box cars in an effort to have a better vantage point with which to effectively hit the fire.

A 4-11 alarm was requested at 4:42 am, which brought a response of five more engine companies and Chief Fire Marshal James Horan who arrived on the fire scene, at 5:05 am. Chief Horan was furious that only one freight door was open to fight this fire, and he ordered the firefighters of Truck Companies 11 and 18 to chop open the remaining doors. Chief Horan then ordered two men to check the condition of the canopy above them. With fire hoses and axes in hand, trapped between the brick building the canopy above them, and the boxcars behind them, the firefighters continued to work. Blinded by the heavy smoke and intense heat, the brave firefighters had no warning other than a deep groan from within the burning structure. Suddenly seven stories of hot molten bricks and timbers came crashing down. The force of the collapse was so great, it not only crushed the canopy, but it knocked several of the boxcars clean off their tracks, and onto their sides.

Twenty-one brave Chicago Firefighters were instantly killed on that very cold winter morning, December 22, 1910. The Stockyards fire shocked the City of Chicago, and the news spread fast across this country regarding the greatest loss of firefighters at a single fire incident anywhere in this nation.

With the very bleak news of their fathers, husbands, brothers, and sons killed the families of the fallen heroes made arrangements to bury their loved ones on Christmas day. A death mask was made of the Chief Fire Marshal James Horan, with the great intention of building a memorial statue for the fallen twenty-one. However, just as many things that are promised to firefighters, this too was never fulfilled. When all the dust settled, and all the smoke cleared away, these brave firefighters unfortunately were forgotten!

PART I

HISTORY OF THE CHICAGO FIRE DEPARTMENT

What type of man does it take to risk his life, and fight the enemy of fire that will never be conquered? We can conquer a human enemy, we can conquer a country, and we can conquer a habit, but we have not been able to conquer fire! Firefighters fight each fire as if it were a battle in war, and when the flames are finally extinguished, and the battle is over, the firefighter returns to the firehouse, and awaits the next alarm, and the next battle.

How did this all begin, and from where did these noble men evolve? Well let's go back through the history of this fire department, and find out just how this noble breed of men, showed such great qualities of high moral character, courage, generosity, honor, strong character and determination.

The volunteer firefighters of Chicago were a special breed of men. In 1832 Chicago was just a frontier village of not more than eight to ten wooden framed buildings. A group of men organized the first fire company called "Washington Volunteers", and they watched over the village day and night. In the summer month of August 5, 1833 the then village of Chicago became incorporated as a town in the state of Illinois.

Chicago at that time had a population of about 150 people. The majority of the town lived on South Water Street, along the southern bank of the Chicago River. The volunteer firemen had a district bounded by Ohio Street on the north, Jackson Street on the south, Jefferson Street on the west, and Lake Michigan which was the boundary on the east side of the town.

The town of Chicago had grown so fast that fire fighting at that time was pretty much a trial and error learning experience. However, they started to become organized teams of men fighting a common enemy "Fire". Hotels and stores were being built faster than anything they ever saw before. To bring in the customers, they had sidewalks constructed of wood to keep the mud in the streets.

The lighting of buildings was done by candles and lanterns, and the heating of buildings by glowing coals or wood. Fire prevention was unheard of at this time. This worried the founding fathers, and as a result, Chicago adopted its first fire ordinance. This ordinance required that all stovepipes passing through the roof must be guarded by tin or iron at least six inches from the wood. A penalty for not protecting the roof was $5, and if the complaint was not fixed within 48 hours, the fine was repeated. Also the new ordinance required every building owner to keep a leather bucket filled with water on the outside if the building contained a stove or a fireplace.

The town authorized the purchase of two fire engines, two ladders, and tools such as, fire hooks, saws, axes, and 1,000 feet of fire hose. The town was then divided into four wards, and a "warden "was appointed for each. One of the first fires recorded in Chicago was at Lake Street and LaSalle Street. Someone had taken a shovel full of hot coals from one stove and was attempting to bring it to his stove, but on the way, he dropped the shovel full of hot coals and a fire occurred. The fire destroyed three houses, a cabinet shop, and a grocery store. The volunteer firemen were praised for their heroic job of extinguishing the fire, but one of the problems was the firemen did not have any one to take charge of the fire. There was no organized discipline or structure to the firemen.

From the days of Benjamin Franklin, who founded the first volunteer Fire Company, it was an honor to become a volunteer firefighter. Often times it opened many new avenues to political positions, and perhaps even a business in those days. Those men who fought fires side by side in the cold winters in Chicago became very close, a "strong camaraderie" was created and they trusted one another with their lives. As a result, the rich and heroic traditions of the fire service evolved.

The volunteer firefighters were ordinary citizens, workmen, city leaders, and wealthy merchants. But at a fire scene they were all firefighters when battling a fire. When they heard the sound of the courthouse bell, the volunteer left his home or his place of work and ran to the engine house.

The first to arrive opened the doors and grabbed a rope under the front axle to start the brakeless engine moving. Others soon arrived and helped pull, and in no time flat the engine was moving fast. Firefighters responded to the station house quickly because the first to arrive had the honor of being the "pipe" man, the person who held the end of the hose. The "pipe" man became a fire department tradition.

Whether the water was obtained from the river, or moved by buckets, pumping it was exhausting work. There were long poles for pumping at both sides of the engine, and a normal cadence was sixty up-and- down strokes per minute. The hardiest of men could work at this speed for only a few minutes. A relief line of men stood by to jump in when the men pumping became tired. Broken fingers and arms were frequent, as the men leaped in to grasp the moving poles without slowing the pace.

On March, 4, 1837, Chicago was incorporated as a city, as the town was growing by leaps and bounds. The buildings were nearly all constructed of wood and other combustible materials. The economy of Chicago was fueled by two factors. The first was the number of city residents that was continually growing. The second reason was that all of the farmers from Northern Illinois and Northwest Indiana did most of their business in Chicago. The population at that time was 4,170, and growing. The fire department also was growing, always trying frantically to keep up with the population by organizing fire companies. The volunteer firefighters took a fierce pride in being called a" Chicago Firefighter."

On Sunday mornings, the volunteers met at the station house to clean and polish the engines, sharpen the axes and pikes, and fill the lamps with oil. Brass fittings were polished to a brilliant shine; wheels, axles, and gears were greased; ropes were checked for fraying; and the fire hose was washed, dried and carefully rewound on the drum to be ready for the next fire

The firemen loved their equipment, and if a new engine or a special piece of equipment was placed into service, a special "christening'" ceremony was held. The engines were painted bright green, red, blue, or yellow, and the volunteers paid money out of their own pockets for many of the trimmings. A certain pride was taken to belong to a fire company.

Nearly all of the city's structures, such as homes, warehouses, stores, and even the sidewalks were constructed of wood, because it was so plentiful. The lumber was cut and transported from Wisconsin and Michigan on barges right down the western shores of Lake Michigan.

Fires were occurring every day, many were small fires, and extinguished right away, but in 1839 a fire broke out at Lake Street and Dearborn, and in no time became a major fire. A building called the Terminate House was totally destroyed, along with seventeen other structures!

The firemen became a special breed set apart from others. As a fire company they started bragging about the fastest lead-outs to the fire, and first to get water on the fire. One thing was for sure, they all risked their lives for their neighbors and it took one hell of a man to get out of his warm bed in the middle of a cold night for his fellow neighbors. At night there were volunteer runners who would carry lamps ahead of the fast moving engine, through the dark streets trying to find the fire.

In November of 1846 the firemen started to give names to their fire companies. Engine Company 4 became the "Red Jackets" and they got their name from wearing one of the first uniforms which consisted of red jackets, white belts and caps. There were rivalries between companies, and most of the time they were not friendly. Two fire companies, the Red Jackets and the Fire Kings made a wager about which company could get to a fire first. The losing fire company had to buy the winners an oyster supper at the St. Charles Hotel.

Chicago's fire companies sponsored social and fund -raising functions. These functions were profitable; one function held by the Washington Company reported raising some $420.00.

As the years went on firefighters were often times injured and became disabled. They then had no way to support themselves or their families. The volunteer firemen created The Firemen's Benevolent Association, which was organized in 1847. Dues for this fund were 50 cents, but then rose to $1.00

Chicago became a good city to find work, and try to make a living. The construction of the Illinois and Michigan Canal was in full swing, and there was a need for cheap labor that many of the newly arriving immigrants could provide. The Irish responded to the call; they were penniless and unskilled, but were very hard workers and were promised ninety cents a day for their work. So with picks, shovels, and mostly by hand, they dug out some ninety-six miles of dirt and clay. The Irish then settled into an area called "Bridgeport," and have remained there to this day and have made it their home.

Chicago Hydraulic Company agreed to let the firefighters use their underground wooden water mains to extinguish fires. This became a great advantage for the firemen, but getting to the water was another story. After locating the water main the firefighters had to dig down to the main, and with their axes they would chop a small hole in the wooden water main. The water would then flow out filling the hole, the firefighter would then begin to fill their buckets, or suction the water up through the hose. When the fire was extinguished, the firefighter would pound a wooden plug into the water main, and mark the location in the event of a future fire. In the year of 1851, fire hydrants began being installed throughout the city of Chicago.

The engine type widely used by the volunteer firefighters was called the "piano box" engine, because it looked like a piano, with the suction for drafting water in the rear of the engine. There was a tool box carried on the engine, with essential tools like an axe, hose spanner, engine wheel wrenches, and even a bed key to take apart beds, so they could be removed from a burning building.

By the year of 1852, the city of Chicago had new boundary lines. The Eastern boundary was Lake Michigan, the Northern boundary was Ohio Street, the western boundary was Clinton Street, and the Southern boundary was Roosevelt Road. Within that south area was very crude working class types of dwellings, and the worst habitations were between State and Clark Streets just north of Roosevelt Road.

Chicago's population was bursting at the seams with now over 200,000 people! The volunteer fire department at this time had ten good working engines; one hook and ladder truck, and some six hose carts. There was about ten thousand feet of hose, but only sixty-five hundred feet of it were in good condition.

A series of festivals were held each year, and one of the last of these festivals took place at the County Fair in Chicago, on October 12, 1857. At these festivals, contest awards were given to the fire company that would throw a stream of water the farthest through 500 feet of fire hose. Because of the fierce competition, the firefighters of engines 3, 4 and 6 had either burst their hose or the air chambers of their engines. Not having their fire hoses available would almost cripple the fire department if a fire were to have occurred before the equipment could be repaired since certainly, fire can and does strike at any time.

In the very early morning hours of October 19, 1857 a group of clerks had been partying all night with some "women of the night" on the second floor of the Hempstead's Wholesale building. During the party a lamp was overturned, and a fast spreading fire occurred. A call was received of a fire at about 4:00am. The location was to 109 – 11 South Water Street. Fanned by high winds the fire spread rapidly in every direction. In a very short time, some of the most costly business structures in the city were totally involved in fire.

As the fire companies arrived on the scene they were almost helpless because of the condition of the Engines, and the busted fire hose that resulted from the competition at the festival on October 12th, as most of the equipment was damaged or crippled. The fire was fought throughout the day, and when it was finally extinguished, 23 lives were lost, and 10 of those were firefighters!

The very first firefighter that was killed in the line of duty was John B. Dickey, Foreman of "Liberty" Hose Company 6. Dickey was leading out a hose line toward the building when suddenly the rear sidewall fell outward, killing him instantly. The greatest loss of life at that fire occurred when a group of merchants and firemen were trying to save the goods on the first floor. Suddenly the roof and the upper floors collapsed, and fell in on them.

Because of the condition of the engines, and the fire hose, and also the manner in which this fire was fought, there was a cry from the businessmen for reform within the fire department. The first thing the business community wanted was new equipment. There was a call for the new steam engine to replace the manual engines that the volunteers used. Even though the volunteers could put out a good stream of water from their manual engines, it was said that the steam engine could send a vertical stream much farther, and was able to continue it for greater lengths of time.

As a direct result of this fire on October 19, 1857, the business men of Chicago called a special meeting. They demanded reform of the fire department and urged acquisition of better equipment, namely the new Steam Engine that was now being used in many other cities. But, the volunteer firefighters were very much opposed to this new steam engine, because of stories they were told about two firefighters being killed after the engine exploded at a fire scene.

The businessmen challenged the volunteers to a test of which piece of equipment could do a better job. The volunteers liked the idea and took the challenge. The volunteers called a meeting at a firehouse where their particular engine was located. They put a line-up together of their best men to insure that they would not fail, and began practicing the rotation, because one man could only take about five minutes of pumping on the manual Engine before he needed a rest.

The news spread fast across Chicago that a new steam engine was being purchased to take on Chicago's volunteer firefighters, who were by then already heroes to the citizens of Chicago. The big day came, and now more than 2500 spectators showed up to watch the big event. The volunteers marched proudly into the courtyard with their manual engine, with thirty of their best men. From the other end of the courtyard, only four men, and four horses pulled the new strange looking steam engine in to place. The time for the test was now!

The two Engines were connected to a water supply. The volunteers showed their ability to get a stream of water faster than the steam engine, and the people cheered! But when the match lit the fuel at the bottom of the boiler of the steam engine, with only cold water in the coil, steam was generated in minutes, and a stream of water was shooting from the nozzle at the end of 400 feet of hose. Pumping at about 160 gallons per minute, the thirty volunteers pumped vigorously to keep their stream higher and farther. With a large amount of black smoke pouring out the top the Steam Engine it began to pump a stream of water over an incredible 225 feet, and higher than a four story building! As the steam engine continued to throw this large stream of water, even the volunteers were shocked. After all of their hard work they still were unable to throw a stream as far or as high. The results of the test exceeded all expectations, and the businessmen were convinced that the Steam Engine could do a better job of extinguishing fires.

The volunteers were still very outspoken about the new steam engine, because they saw it as a beginning of the volunteer's extinction. Shortly after the test in the courtyard, the first steam engine was purchased by the city of Chicago. After hearing the news about the purchase, the volunteer firefighters became very angry, and they marched on the courthouse in protest. The mayor ordered the police to arrest any disorderly firefighters, but no arrests were made.

This was the beginning of the end of the old volunteer fire department in Chicago. The new steam engines began to replace the manual pumping engines one by one. This was very similar to what the locomotive did to the stagecoach. But let it be said, that the Chicago volunteer firefighters, were as fine a set of men that ever responded to a fire, and in the finest traditions of the fire service. They were tough, brave and skillful.

As time went on, the volunteer fire companies began to disband. Hope Hose Company, the last volunteer fire company held a meeting, and decided to disband, and it was a very sad day for the proud, Hope Hose Company. In doing so they marked the end of an era. The Hope Hose Company sold their engine, and all the proceeds were given to the home of the friendless.

On August 2, 1858, the City Council passed an ordinance that made way for the organizing of an all-paid fire department in the city of Chicago.

Firefighters were to be paid twenty-five dollars per month for all rank and file members. Denis Swenie was elected Chief Engineer of the paid department. Swenie began his fire career as a runner when he joined volunteer company 3 "The Niagara", which was located at Kinzie and Wells Streets.

Even though Swenie was a young man he knew how to begin putting things in order on the fire department. He demonstrated excellent organizational skills. One of the first things Swenie had to do was to get the first steam engine in service. He needed to get men he trusted such as firemen he worked with before, and it did not take him long before he had all of them. The new Engine was called "Long John" and was put into service at Franklin and Adams Streets. The four horses that would pull this big engine were stored in a stable about four blocks away. Very soon after the new engine company was put into service a tragic fire occurred, and the deaths of some nine people were blamed on the response time of the new engine. As a result, a stable was added on to the rear of the firehouse, and the horses were now relocated with the steam engine.

Later that same year, three more steam engines were purchased by the city, and they were named: Enterprise, Atlantic, and the Island Queen. Along with the steam engines horses were purchased by the city. There was a need for drivers, not just any drivers however, they had to be team drivers that could seize the reins and talk in a way to the four horses that would then lead them to a fire scene.

Chief Engineer Swenie's next objective was to bring harmony back to the fire department. Many of the volunteers who wanted to be on the paid department were told that they must conform to the rules or quit the fire service. Every firefighter on duty was required to wear a badge and a uniform, and no engine was to be used unless it belonged to the city. Many of the volunteers opposed the rules, but the fire department held its own during those first stormy days, and the new fire department organization began to meld well.

On March 4, 1861, Abraham Lincoln was elected as this Nation's Sixteenth President. Lincoln not only built a strong Republican Party; he also rallied most of the northern Democrats to the Union's cause. Shortly after the election, on April 12, 1861, the Confederate Army attacked the Union garrison at Fort Sumter. The War Between the States was ignited, which had been anticipated for a long time. The South, with a white population of 5.5 million people, had to face the North with some 20 million people.

The volunteer firefighters of Chicago began joining the Union Army as groups. They fought the war as finely and courageously as they fought fires side by side. With the all-paid fire department now being formed in Chicago, those who opposed the department went to fight Johnny Reb. Denis Swenie was only in command of the Chicago Fire department for one year. He was replaced by Silas Mc Bride, however he was not considered fully competent to head a large fire department.

In February 1863 the city was divided into 16 wards, and the Chief Engineer of the fire department, and the First and Second Assistant Engineers were now elected by the people of the city of Chicago.

But even in the midst of death and desolation from the Civil War, people in Chicago still worked, ate, and slept. Everyday life for civilians went on much as the usual pace and the fire department continued to put engine companies into service. A new telegraph wire was strung from New York City to San Francisco, reducing the communication time between the two coasts, from days to now just seconds!

Before the War Between the States there was no meat industry in Chicago. As in other cities, Chicago's local meat needs were provided by many competing stockyards. The civil war changed that in no time. With more than a million men in uniform the Union Army demanded processed meat. Chicago answered the call to feed the Union Army, and with Chicago's great railroad network that reached far and wide, they did feed the army and many, many more people. By 1863, Chicago was the largest Meatpacking City in the world, and became known as the world's "hog butcher".

Not only had Chicago become the largest meat packing city, but Chicago also dominated the lumber market for high quality lumber. Now with the Illinois and Michigan Canal in full use, the amount of lumber that passed through the city had doubled. The city of Chicago was booming, and many changes were being made to keep up with its population growth.

A" Board of Control" was formed in Chicago, to establish the new paid fire department. A budget was prepared for new fire department equipment, salaries, and supplies. New firehouses were being erected to accommodate the large steam engines. The board also had to improve the water system, because the steam engines needed larger water mains. The city council also passed a resolution for a committee to look into the cost of constructing a telegraph system in Chicago, to speed up the alarm response time for fire calls.

The Firemen's Benevolent Association raised money for needy members who had been injured or disabled as a result of fighting fires. In 1864, some six years after the volunteer companies were officially disbanded and replaced by the paid department; the Association purchased an 80 x 90 foot plot in the Rosehill Cemetery on Chicago's north side where stands a 35 foot marble shaft, with a statue of a firefighter on the top.

This monument commemorates the 15 fire brigade members that are buried there in that particular plot.

On April 9, 1865, the War Between the States ended with the surrender by Confederate General Robert E. Lee at Appomattox. The war with all of its glory, and valor, and the tragic loss of 600,000 dead, will always be remembered as a terrible time in our Nation's history. Just five days after the surrender, on Good Friday April 14, 1865, President Lincoln was assassinated by John Wilkes Booth at the Ford Theatre in Washington D.

C. Booth was a stage actor who somehow thought he was helping the South by committing this terrible crime.

The Board of Control's Committee found that the price of a new fire alarm system would cost $70,000 for 125 miles of wires, 106 Alarm Boxes, 14 engine house gongs, 6 bell strikers, and the office fixtures in the Central Fire Communications Office. On the second of June, the system was formally turned over to the city. The Central Fire Communications Office was still located in the courthouse in the cupola.

There were many stockyards scattered throughout Chicago. The Chicago Pork Packers Association and the nine railroads had a historic conference, in an effort to consolidate the meat packing industry. They purchased a one half square mile tract of land four miles south of downtown Chicago. The land was not very good land, and most of it was swampland. The land was owned by the former Mayor "Long John Wentworth" and was sold for the sum of one hundred thousand dollars. The Association then devised a way to drain away swamp water right into the south branch of the Chicago River. This track of land was located between Halsted Street on the East, and Ashland Avenue on the West, from 39th street on the North to 47th Street on the South. On December 25th, 1865, the New Union Stockyards opened in that location.

As the years progressed, so did the city of Chicago. Buildings were being built much higher than fire department ladders could reach. Firefighters needed newer and faster ways to reach the higher floors of these buildings that were now amazingly, four and five stories high! By 1866, the Chicago Fire Department had 11 engine companies in service, 2 hand engines, but only one Hook and Ladder Truck Company. There were now 120 paid members, 125 volunteers, and 53 horses.

The layout of a typical firehouse had the steam engine in the center of the ground floor. In front of the engine was the Supply Hose Cart. The floors were constructed of wood planking, and behind the engine were the stable doors where the horses were kept in stalls. The second floor had a hay loft in the rear, and a small bunk room in front for the firefighters.

The duties of a fireman when he was not fighting a fire were many. Some of the most important, were to take good care of the engine, the horses, and most important, take good care of your Foremen. The interior of the firehouse was spotless, and everything in the building had its proper place, and it had better be there! Very strict rules were in effect, so that when a fire occurred, all would be ready to respond. This was the discipline and team work that had worked so well in the fire services short proud history!

The life of firefighting and dedication to saving lives and property was something only a very few men wished to undertake. It had to be a person with great courage, generosity, physical strength, and honor, to become a member of the Chicago Fire Department.

PART II

The story of the Chicago Fire Department from 1866 until the fire of Dec. 22, 1910 when the Fallen 21 Firemen were killed in the Chicago Stockyards Fire told by a fictitious fireman named, Norman Doolan.

My name is Norman Doolan, and I am a new firefighter in the city of Chicago. The Engine Company that I have been assigned to is Engine 6, the "Little Giant" located at 514 West Maxwell Street. I had been working as a carpenter with my uncle, but the only job I ever wanted was to be a Chicago fireman. Chicago has been organizing fire companies with the paid department for the past few years, and I waited for my turn to join. I volunteered to help at many fires, and have always worked hand and hand with firefighters; I always asked if they needed firefighters to please consider me. Finally one night after a big fire in 1867, a chief called me over, and asked me if I was still interested in being a firefighter. I replied, "You bet I am, very interested."

I met the men of Engine 6, the "Little Giant" as this engine company was called they were a close bunch; many of them had been volunteers before the paid department began. The Foreman of the company was sitting at his desk. His name is William Musham and he is a man that adheres to the strict rules of the Department. Ed Jennings is the Company Engineer, and he has about the most experience in running steam engines as anyone on the job. The pipe man is a guy called John O'Rourke, he is a seasoned veteran of the fire department, and has gone to many fires. He is an experienced man who is willing to teach the younger firefighters the many tricks of the trade, if they want to learn. He was a great training asset, especially for me.

The big steam engine is parked off to one side, just behind the supply hose cart, with two very large wheels. There is a large coffee pot sitting on top of a black cast iron wood burning stove, along the west wall of the fire house. Off to the side there is a sitting area with five chairs, and just behind that area, is a wall with three doors that lead into the stable, where five horses are kept in stalls.

In the morning, there are many things that need to be done to assure that everything is ready for the next fire alarm. One of the first things was to make sure that the steam engine is ready; plenty of dry shavings and kindling wood is in the furnace. The water level should be between the second and third gauge cock. Every part of the engine should be thoroughly examined, whether it has been worked at a fire or not. Normally that's the engineer's job, but Musham wants everyone in this house to know how to get this engine in service, and ready to go to a fire.

The drivers of the engine and the hose cart take care of the horses. They will take special care of keeping them fed and clean, and healthy. Firefighters are responsible for the cleanliness of company quarters, and see to it that the sitting area, bunk room, and stables are kept scrupulously clean and neat. Also, any other chores in the fire house that the Foreman, Bill Musham, can think of, was given to the candidate fireman ---- ME!

Once the house work was finished, the horses had to be exercised, especially if they had not performed any work within the last twenty-four hours. The drivers, with the assistance of the other firefighters, would lead the five horses out onto Maxwell Street in front of the fire house. Exercising consisted of a slow trot, from one end of the block to the other end. The people always stopped to watch the fire horses, because they were special. Unlike milk and ice wagon horses, that was just basic horses fire horses were the best of their breed. They were very fast, agile, strong and intelligent. Two of the horses were"Percherons", and two were "Morgans". They were the horses that pulled the steam engine. The horse that pulled the supply hose cart was a" Belgiandraft" horse, and he also was very strong. All the horses were kept with their harnesses on at all times, to insure a fast push out to a fire.

After exercising the horses they were returned to their clean stalls and dried off with a good rub down. After the horses are fed and watered, the Foreman William Musham would assign the hours for meals to the firemen for the day. Each man is allowed three hours each day for meals at separate times. The firefighters will leave and eat their meals, and return so the next man could leave for his meal. In all cases when leaving company quarters, all members would make an entry into the Company Journal, stating the reason for leaving, and the exact time that they returned to duty.

The Company Journal is like the "Bible" of the fire house, if you will. Everyday a complete record of all transactions and operations of the men, equipment, and fire calls must be accurately documented in the Company Journal.

In the late evening hours of September 9th, we were all sitting around in the back of the firehouse, when the gong began to clang. The new telegraph alarm system gave a Box number, and if that number appears on the board in the firehouse, then that fire company would respond to that Box alarm address. The firemen were running toward the front and the Foreman yells, "That's us," and rings the firehouse bell. The horses are very restless, because they know at the sound of the bells they soon would be hitched -up to the engine and hose wagon. The second round of bells begins. That's Box 2-6-4 at Lake Street and Franklin Street. The stall doors swung open and the horses quickly move into place in front of the engine. Let's go hook them up Mushan yells, as the firemen tighten the girths from under the horses. Then engineer Jennings applies the torch to the dry shavings in the furnace, as the drivers climb up into their seats. The two big station doors swing open, and the driver yells to the lead horse," Geee –Yaah!" The supply hose cart begins to move out onto Maxwell Street, followed by the Steam Engine. The excited horses are kicking, and snorting through their nostrils. As they are pulling, and getting their footing, the driver yanks the reins to the right, and the horses turn east up Maxwell Street. Their hooves send dirt and dust flying out in all directions.

As they approached the corner of Maxwell and Canal Streets, the driver yanks the reins to the left, and the lead horses begin turning left onto Canal Street. He stands up yelling "Yaah – Yaah, get'em up". The horses begin to kick up speed going north to Roosevelt Road, where they turned left about one block to Jefferson Street where they make a sharp right turn. With tails streaming out behind them, and their sleek bodies heaving, every muscle working, the horses were in a full gallop.

In the distance the firefighters could see heavy smoke and flying embers in the air."We got a working fire," the driver yelled. "Come – on, come – on, kick them feet," as the horses strained at the leather collars around their large necks. As they approached Lake Street, the powerful Steam Engine was belching smoke out of the stack, and Musham directed his driver to go over the river, and secure the fire hydrant at the corner of Franklin and Lake Streets. As they pulled up to the hydrant, the horses were panting heavily after the long run. Firefighters jumped from the back step of the engine and hose cart, they began to take down the hard suction hose from the side, and began hooking it to the hydrant. As the hose cart pulls up in front of the burning building, the firefighters begin stretching the hose, and Musham begins to size this fire up. The fire is in a three-story wooden warehouse in the center of the block, the Foreman directs the pipe man O'Rouke to lead – out the hose to the east side of the burning structure.

There is an entrance into the first floor on the eastside of the burning building, with a stairway leading up to the second floor. But, it appears that most of the heat and smoke was coming up from the cellar stairway on the left. The engineer, Ed Jennings, shouted, "Here comes your water"."Get your hands on that line," Musham yelled to his candidate. O'Rourke begins stretching the hose line inside the first floor doorway, but he can't get in too far because the fire is to his left in the stairway leading down to the cellar.

He begins to hit the fire straight on with the water, and starts moving toward the stairs. The Chief arrives, and orders two more hose lines to be led-out, one around the rear of the structure, and the other on the side to one of the cellar windows. Truck Company 2 starts opening windows on the first and second floors to ventilate the smoke and in no time at all the fire begins to produce large amounts of white and gray smoke. The Chief knows that the firefighters are getting water on the fire.

Back in the stairway, Engine 6 is inching their way down to the cellar, but for every step they are taking a terrible beating, choking and coughing, from the heat and smoke. There is a hose line shooting water through the west window that is pushing the fire right on the men of engine 6. The Foreman, Musham, yells to the company in the window to shut their pipe down because we are now down in the cellar. O'Rourke hands me the pipe, as he leaves for a breath of fresh air. With my foreman at my side we are crawling on the cellar floor, playing the engine stream on the burning floor joists above him. We are moving in further and my foreman tells me in a reassuring voice, "We have got to get that fire over there in the corner." Soon O'Rourke returns, and gives me a much needed brake on the line, as we advance the line through the cellar. The firefighters from truck 2 begin to pull down the overhead ceiling, and overhaul the contents of the cellar. The Chief enters into the hot cellar to see how the progress is going, and Musham informs the Chief that we got this one under control. "Good job, guys," the Chief replies!

The Foreman of Engine Company 5 tells his engineer to shut down the pumps, and stand – by, as they walk around the rear of the building. Although the fire caused heavy damage to the rear, it had been stopped before extending to the wood framed structure to the east. The Chief and the firefighters are a little overcautious, as they check for any more fire. They begin to open walls where the fire may have traveled up through the flooring and between the studs. This is very necessary work. The firefighters must be thorough, because after they leave the fire scene, they don't want to have to return because of a "rekindle" that could be worse than the initial fire.

The Chief gave the orders to finish the wash down on the first floor, and says, "Let's pick – up the fire hose, because this fires out". The engines are shutting down one by one, and the hoses are all being picked up, and the ladders are put back on the truck. They hitched the horses up again, and all the fire companies return to their respective fire houses.

The Chicago Fire department now had some fourteen engine companies in service. But, this was just not enough to keep up with the growing population. Planning was almost impossible, but the Chicago Fire Department held meetings almost everyday to adopt running assignments of the new engine companies. Because of a divided administration the fire department constantly hassled with the board of police, and the city council to get anything accomplished. After many long hours they concluded that the alarm of the fire response would be from the Central Fire Alarm Office in the court house copula. The response would be as follows:

Upon the first fire call, three or four engine companies would be dispatched to the alarm. When the second fire call was requested, four more engine companies were dispatched also from the Fire Alarm Office to the fire scene. When a third alarm was requested all remaining engine companies in the city would then respond to the fire. The saying engine company "Still Alarm "meant that a fire had been discovered by a fire company, and this term meant an alarm was not sounded on the city wide fire house gongs or bell circuits. New firefighters were entering the department all the time, and the manning of fire companies was very important. But, as usual the police board and the city council were always trying to keep the fire departments budget down. A report came out from the Chief Fire Marshal, U.P. Harris, that many firefighters have been injured as a result of fighting fires. On April 13th one firefighter of Hook & Ladder Company 9, Michael Burns, suffocated from smoke and died as he attempted to rescue two small children.

This report did not stop any new construction in the city; hotels were being built to house all the visitors that were coming into Chicago. Many were built around the loop area or downtown near the Board of Trade, and the court house. These hotels were for all attorneys, and business man who traveled into Chicago, and they were the best in town. There were also many new hotels built near the railroad station. A very nice hotel room included the following, a kerosene lamp, bed, chair and a small cast iron stove which added elegance to the room.

Yes, Chicago had the most hotels, the tallest grain elevators, the largest stores, and fancy homes. As a matter of fact Chicago was almost completely constructed of wood. The number of structures in the city at this time was 48,867, and of that number 44,274 were wooden structures. The construction of these structures was haphazard at most, and not just here and there, large sections of the city were no more than wooden boxes. There was no attention being given to fire prevention, and that was almost scary in the eyes of a firefighter. The growing population brought so much congestion of people trying to get from one place to another, so the citizens asked for some type of cheap transportation. A new corporation devised away to move the people around Chicago by way of a horse-car-line. The horse- car-line ran along State Street, between 12th Street on the south and Lake Street on the north. This horse-car-line worked so well that it began to expand in all directions of the city and in just a few years a person could travel from the loop area to the Stockyards at 4000 South Halsted Street with ease. The horse-car was mostly for inter-city people who worked in and around Chicago, and it provided good transportation.

But, what put Chicago on the map were the railroads. By the end of 1867, an incredible four thousand miles of railroad track led and were connected to Chicago. Some one hundred and fifty trains entered and left Chicago each day. When an incident occurred on the railroads they called the fire department for help. Another winter had set in, and by the end of January everything in Chicago was frozen. January is a time when you stay indoors, and you don't go outside unless you have a good reason. It had been a slow stretch for the firemen working at Engine Company 1, and Truck Company 1. The fire house is located at 121 south LaSalle Street; the structure was a two story brick building with the outside dimensions of 44 x80 feet. The foreman of Engine 1 was Joel Kinney, and the foreman of Truck 1 was George Ernst. Both men are seasoned veterans on the job with many fires under their belts, and both were with the volunteers. The firefighters had spent their shift cleaning most of the day interrupted only by sporadic false alarms.

The first floor of this firehouse had two bays, one for the engine and hose cart, and one for the truck. There were three black cast iron wood/coal burning stoves that heated the first floor. The coffee was always hot, and kept on the back stove close to the sitting area.

Firemen talked about every thing, you name it and they talked about that subject until something else came up. But, most of all they talked about fires, and their equipment. They talked a lot about the horses, and the work they performed for the firemen. All the equipment of the Chicago Fire Department was pulled by horses. Engines, hook & ladders, hose carts, supply wagons, and the chief's buggy all had assigned horses.

Each horse upon assignment will have a descriptive card containing the date of purchase, age of horse, color and name. Each horse is fitted with a prescribed collar, and like engineer Jennings says, "You take good care of the horses, and they will take care of you when they have to perform their duties".

It was in the very early morning hours on January 28th, 1868, and Firefighter Mulvey, a young firefighter and a friend of mine had the floor watch at Engine 1/Truck 1's firehouse. The men were asleep, the horses were in their stalls and firefighter Mulvey had stoked up the fires in two of the stoves and was adding wood to the third when suddenly the gong sounded. Firefighter Mulvey ran to the front of the firehouse to check the Box and number that was ringing. The Box alarm was located at Lake Street and Wabash Avenue, and Mulvey soon knew that this Box was for Engine 1 and Truck Company 1. The bells began ringing throughout the firehouse. The first man down the stairs was the foreman, Joel Kinney, and he began yelling," Let's get going, get those harnesses on the horses." Within minutes they were all hitched, and moving out the front doors of the fire house. First the hose cart then the engine followed by the hook & ladder. They galloped at a fast pace across downtown Chicago. Upon their arrival on the scene there was heavy smoke and a fire condition; fire was issuing from a three-story wood framed building on all floors. Engine 1 secured a hydrant on the corner of Lake Street, the engineer and driver began to connect to the hydrant, and drop the trace chains from the horses.

The firefighters of the hose company laid about 400 feet of 2 ½ inch hose to the engine that was soon hooked up, and the engineer yelled, "Here comes your water." Finally, in what seemed to be hours but was only minutes, the firefighters had their water and had a powerful stream of water that was now playing on the burning structure as more engine companies were arriving on the scene setting up and leading out their hose lines. The Chief gave orders to concentrate their streams on the exposures so the fire would not extend any farther. The original fire building was now fully involved in fire and began to collapse, but not before igniting many other structures. Engine Company 6 was ordered to advance our line up into the structure to the south which now had fire on the second floor.

As we fought the fire from room to room in their structure the other fire companies had some six fire streams working on the five buildings that surrounded this extra alarm fire. Up on the second floor my Foreman, Bill Musham, is yelling his ass off for me, but that's not new to me; he is always yelling. "Doolan, get in here," he yelled. "I yelled back, "I'm coming I'm coming already, easy on the whip I am only a hired horse, boss." I have two and half years on the job and he still yells at me. O'Rourke handed me the pipe, and said, "Get some time on the job kid, and he won't yell as much". Musham and I continue working the line down the hallway beating down the flames. All at once it became much easier to breathe, because the smoke was venting out the end gable of the roof. The roof and end gable had collapsed, and most of the fire was extinguished. Soon the words I have been waiting for, "Engine Company 6, pick-up, you're going home," the chief yelled. After many hours the fire was finally brought under control. The damage from this fire was huge with a loss of over one and a half million dollars.

Picking- up from a fire is a lot of work, but we were glad to be going back to the fire house so soon. O'Rourke said that he thought we would be here until at least noon. Fireman Musham gives the order to start picking up the hose from the nozzle end first, and we will work toward the engine, keeping a flow of water in the hose because the temperature is below freezing.

Everyone helps roll the frozen hose, and puts it up on the hose wagon. Once we get to the engine Jennings will detach the suction from the engine, and then detach it from the hydrant. Musham says, "Throw the two bags of coal up on the engine and the rest left in the street will have to be shoveled up onto the supply wagon."Doolan says, "Hey I think it is easer to put the fire out, than it is to put all this stuff back on the rig, and the hose cart." They hitched the horses back up, and begin returning to quarters.

Once the engine is back inside the fire house there is much to do, and everyone works until the engine is back in service and ready for a fire. The fire hose is washed, and hung in the hose tower to dry. The drivers will take care of the horses; they will provide new bedding in the stalls, and water right away. All the horses are dried off, and rubbed down after returning from a fire. The engineer will clean out the furnace, and prepare it for fuel. First he will place two large pieces of wood on each side of the grate, then about a half a bushel of shavings, and then he fills the furnace with light dry wood in a criss-cross manner in layers. Jennings then checks the water level in the boiler, and now this steam engine is back in service ready for the next fire.

The Chicago Fire Department continued to expand with the city, and new rules and regulations were being written almost every day. The battalion chief and his driver, who was called "Buggyman", would show up at Engine 6's house at around 10:00 am as he made his daily rounds from one engine house to another. The chief always had some type of new orders with him, and he would give them to the Foreman explaining to him what they were all about.

The buggyman would come in the back with the firemen, and he always had some stories about the job. Some of the stories were true, but most were just scuttle-butt that he overheard from one chief talking to another. Often times the chief would come in the back, and have coffee with us. This day he informed us that the new orders that he brought just might be the last orders by our beloved Chief Fire Marshal, U.P. Harris. The word is that he got ill at that last fire we had on Lake Street, and he has not felt good ever since. What will this job do without Chief Harris?" O'Rourke said. Musham walked over, poured a cup of coffee and said, "as much as we all idolized Chief Harris this job will always go on, because no one man alone makes this job".

The Chief also informed us that the groundwork for improving the water supply system was well on its way. Over a year ago the engineers completed digging a five foot diameter tunnel through clay some sixty feet below the lake level. The tunnel was lined with two shells of bricks, and went about two miles off shore. An intake crib was built of timber, and will be connected to a pumping station at Chicago Avenue by sometime next year. This new water system will make fire fighting a lot easier, and that's a good thing for us.

The Foreman, William Musham, was a stickler about the new orders, and wanted to make sure we all new what they meant. So he said, "Pull up a chair boys, because I want to read these new orders we got today". The new orders stated

1. All members of the Chicago Fire Department are always on duty for the purpose of discipline
2. Members shall not enter into places where intoxicating liquors are sold while in the garb of the department uniform.
3. Every member of the fire department shall wear his prescribed uniform, and wear his badge and insignia.
4. When a member leaves company quarters for his meals his uniform will always be buttoned up and will be neat and clean.

"Hey Boss, what do these new orders mean?" I asked. "Well Norm, rules are made because someone did something wrong. In this case he probably was in uniform in a saloon, and the uniform was dirty and unbuttoned". Then the Foreman said, "get done with the housework, and I will work on the meal assignments".

"Oh, I see what you mean about the rules," Doolan says, "we break them, and they make them right," as he walks toward the horse stalls in the back of the fire house. Musham laughed a little to himself. That's just about right.

Rusty's Grill was at the corner of Maxwell Street and Canal Street about a half-a-block from the fire house. Most of the firefighters ate their meals there, because Rusty probably made the best fried potatoes in Chicago, and also if you ate your meals there he gave you the fireman's discount. The regular three square meals for most firemen were breakfast: steak, fried potatoes, eggs and hot bread followed by some pancakes topped with molasses. The noon meal included roast beef, vegetables and pie or pudding for dessert. The supper meal was usually like breakfast, but without the eggs and pancakes. No matter what you ate at Rusty's you went back to the fire house fully satisfied.

On April 2, 1868 the Chief Fire Marshal, U.P. Harris resigned; he was replaced by Chief Robert Williams, and Engine Company 11 was put into service at 10 East Hubbard Street with Captain Larry Walsh was the Foreman. One of the first fires that Engine 11 responded to on March 11, 1869 was a warehouse fire at the Wisdorn Plaining Mill located at 34 – 36 North Canal Street. At that alarm four brave firefighters, Pipemen George Bergh, Thomas O'Brien, Charles Wilt, and Peter Marrotta were killed on the roof of the structure after a total collapse.

Construction was completed on the Pumping Station at Michigan Avenue & Chicago Avenue and it was activated. Large water mains were dug under the river that would be connected to three large water reservoirs, one in each division of the city. Three more engine companies were put into service in the city, one on the west side, and two at the south end of the city. By 1870 fire protection was getting much better with the easy access to a good water supply and the steady increase in fire companies.

But Chicago at this time was all about the railroads, and that put Chicago on the map. The railroads had built insulated rail cars that they filled with ice, and the G.H. Hammond Company began shipping beef longer distances, because they could preserve the meat. The Union Stockyards now consisted of some twenty-three hundred pens, and meat packing houses such as Swift and Armor, were conveniently located adjacent to the stockyards. The railroads brought in the farmers harvest on time; it was all about money and timing. Chicago's market paid top dollar for the golden grain of Illinois, and then in came the "Mechanical Reaper" that could cut two acres of wheat per hour. A farmer could bring his harvest to market quickly, because of this new mechanical reaper and the railroads. For many years, farmers cut stalks of grain by hand with sickles. The stalks were bound into bundles stacked together, and left in the field until they could be threshed. All the grain had to be cut within about ten days after ripening, or it spoiled. A farmer could cut and band about one acre of grain per day. This Mechanical Reaper was pulled by two horses, as the reaper moved forward; a wheel rolled along the ground, and drove its moving parts. In the front of the reaper a vibrating blade about four and a half feet long cut the grain.

The railroads had very easy access to the stockyards pulling right up to the pens. The Union Stockyards contained three miles of water troughs, ten miles of feed troughs for its livestock, and nearly thirty miles of drainage pipes carried the stockyards waste right into the Chicago River's South Branch which soon became known as "Bubbly Creek," because it was so polluted. Business men and visitors from all over the world were coming into Chicago, because of the fast growth, that was so amazing to people. Chicago had the lumber industry, the meat industry, the farming industry, and the railroad industry all in one city. People from Europe made statements about this great city like, "I wish I could go back to America if only to see Chicago," they said. "This city seems to consist mainly of shops and stores. People come here to trade and make money, but not to live." Another said, "This whole dam city is mad after money!" All these visitors were right about one thing, Chicago was a city where people of all groups could and did make money, but they were wrong about the other thing, people did live here, and raised their family's here, it is a grand place to live.

By the year of 1871, Chicago rail routes were into some six states, and began to revolutionize commerce in Chicago by expanding the areas that city merchants controlled. This market was said to be unlimited. This is a city, not in growth, but in revolution. "The word growth is much to slow a word for what is happening in Chicago," one visitor said. "By God they've even turned the Chicago River to flow to the west, so not to pollute that beautiful Lake Michigan that Chicago sits on."

"Yes, the city was still growing, but at a faster pace than the Chicago Fire Department could keep up with," Musham told Doolan. Just yesterday the Chiefs were before the board requesting more equipment, engines, fire hose, and most of all manpower. The city was now over 36 square miles, and was just too spread out for only sixteen engine companies.

"You can say anything you want to about this matter," O'Rourke said, "but all this money and all this growth in Chicago should be good for the department, right?"

Because of a divided administration on the fire department things couldn't be worse. The control of the fire department was divided between the Board of Police, who administered the Chicago Fire Department, and the City Council who appropriates the money.

The fire departments chief officers continually made proposals, but to no avail since the board thought and believed that the fire department budget had to be kept down, because it was already costing too much money to have firemen sitting around all day doing nothing!

On June 2nd 1871, the sad news came out, that our beloved Chief U.P. Harris had passed away. This guy was not just a chief officer, he was one of the boys, and in fact his nick-name was" Boy Fireman" by many of his close friends. On the volunteer department, he served as Chief Engineer, and when the department became an all paid department, U.P. Harris was elected Chief of the Brigade. He was idolized by the firefighters who worked for him. When he arrived on the scene of a fire the men fought harder and longer to extinguish the fire than for any other chief on the job. His funeral was one of the largest in Chicago, hundreds of his admirers attended, and his pall bearers were all firefighters that he worked with.

The summer of 1871 was very hot, and dry. Warmer than any that Bill Musham and any of the other firefighters remember. For over two and a half months almost no rain had fallen in the Chicago area.

In the early evening hours of September 30th, a watchman high up in the court house cupola sighted some smoke and flames toward the southeast section of the city. He turned in the alarm just south of Roosevelt Road, on State Street. Within minutes firefighters from three engine companies were dispatched to the fire and also one hook & ladder company on that very hot evening.

Upon their arrival on the scene, fire was racing up the south interior stairway of the structure. Firefighters began leading out hose, and gaining entry into the burning structure. Ben McCarthy, Fire Warden of the south division immediately requested a second alarm, at 16th and State Streets. The structure involved was a five-story heavy wood timbered warehouse, and because of the very hot dry conditions in a short time the fire was through the roof.

The second assistant, Chief Loranz Walters arrived on the scene and saw thick heavy smoke billowing out the east and north sides of the structure. Fire was now visible through the roof so Chief Walters requested a third alarm and all remaining engines began responding to the fire.

Firefighters advanced their lines up a stairway to the second floor. Heavy smoke forced them to their knees as they fought the flames in a long hallway. The fire was now issuing from window openings on the east side of the building. Being fanned by a fourteen mile an hour wind from the southwest, the flames were licking the sides of an adjoining five-story warehouse. The brave firefighters were leading out fire hose to the east side of the burning structure in an effort to stop this inferno from extending to the second warehouse The battle went on throughout the night, and to about mid-morning. After this long fight the Burlington warehouse "A" was a total loss, but by the fine efforts of the Chicago Firefighters warehouse "B" was saved. There were over two million dollars worth of teas, coffee, and sugar that was stored in warehouse "B".

In the newspapers almost everyday there were stories about major forest fires in Michigan, Wisconsin, and Illinois. Sometimes in the late afternoon you could see the smoke in the distance from Chicago, and it just added to the growing discomfort, of that very strange summer weather for firemen. There was not much rest for the Chicago firemen, it seemed like there was a big fire almost everyday that first week of October, with temperatures in the 80's. People who lived in Chicago were looking forward to autumn, because it usually began getting cooler and rainier, but not this year.

The Chicago Tribune newspaper had just moved into their new fireproof buildings, but they were very uneasy about the building around their new structure that were not fireproof buildings. In an editorial that hot summer of 1871 the Tribune warned that the city's fancy marble fronts of many of the downtown buildings were just a thin veneer. Many structures were almost a hundred feet in height, with a single bricks thickness, and when a fire burns in this type of structure, the wooden wall that holds the bricks burns away leaving tons of bricks swaying in the breeze just waiting to fall.

The Chicago firefighters knew that if a fire began in one of those structures, that it could cause serious injury, collapsing and falling outward, not only killing citizens, but also firefighters. No one wanted to hear what the firemen had to say, and they just kept building this same type of hazardous and flimsy construction everywhere in downtown Chicago.

On Saturday October 7th in the early evening some of Chicago's firefighters were still working at fires cleaning up the remaining burning embers of the fires that raged the day before on Des Plaines Street. But, most of the fire companies were now back in service across the city, and all they could talk about was trying to get some much needed rest. Not only were the firemen in need of rest, but so were the horses who pulled the engines from one fire to the next in the past week. Doolan walked through the stable doors in the rear of the fire house. Two of the horses were lying down in their stalls, and Ed Jennings was giving more water to his favorite horse "Dunkin". Jennings said, "You know a horse drinks about eight gallons of water a day, but I think Dunkin here has drank about ten gallons today." "Yeah, and I know why. It's because of this dry weather were having in Chicago. We need rain, and a lot of it," Norm said. Ed finished giving Dunkin the water, and went upstairs. Doolan had the floor watch until 1:00 am.

Saturday Night Fire

Somewhere just after 10:30 pm, an unknown person let a fire get out of control in the boiler room in the basement of the Lull & Holmes Planning Mill located at 209 South Canal Street. The fire was sighted by the watchman in courthouse cupola. The first alarm was sounded in the west division, and four engines were dispatched to the fire. The First Assistant Chief of the Brigade, John Schank, spotted the flames, and turned up Canal Street toward the fire. By the time he arrived on the scene, the fire had extended out of the basement and up the south side of the Mill and was burning out of control.

Chief Schank went down Adams Street, west to Clinton Street, and after sizing up the fire he immediately requested a general alarm, from the street Box 248. This fire was so out of control the chief wasn't sure where to set up the incoming engines. As the bells started ringing at Engine company 6, I looked up at the map on the wall, and said to myself "Dam it, that's in the west division again. They are always having trouble," he said as the bells began ringing.

In no time at all the horses were hitched up, and we were going out the doors again. As we turned north on Canal Street you could see a large bright glow in the sky, and that wind was still blowing out of the southwest. As we approached the fire we were met by Chief Loranz Walters, and he ordered us to set-up on the corner of Jackson and Canal Streets.

The chief jumped back on his buggy and headed west down Jackson Street. The wind was a main factor tonight, blowing hot embers toward the northeast, but the radiant heat from the fire was still igniting the wooden dwellings and out buildings west of the main fire toward Clinton Street. In a very short time, about twenty minutes or so, the northern three quarters of this square block was fully engulf in flames that were reaching over fifty feet in the air. Chief Williams, the Chief of the Brigade moved most of the engine companies to the corner of Canal and Adams Streets.

"We need to set up a water curtain right here so we don't lose anymore buildings to the north," Williams said. About seven engines were set up with over ten engine streams now directed on both sides of Adams Street. "Somehow we have to stop this fire right here or we could lose the whole dam city of Chicago," the Chief said.

Engine companies were pumping from the river and from hydrants just east of Canal Street, hose lines were stretched to the south and to the west. As the fierce flames approached the Canal Street side, firefighters bravely stood their ground. Each man took his turn on the pipe with burning embers landing all around them. Often times a firefighter would fall back to get a fresh breath of air, only to return to fight this inferno. The fire has now jumped over Canal Street, and headed east toward the river. This fire brought terror into the hearts of citizens, who now feared that it might sweep through the city, people began running for their lives. The wall of fire moved swiftly into the wooden houses and barns next to the river bank, and a silhouette appeared through the smoke and flames. It was hook & ladder 1, "Pioneer" engulfed in flames after the collapse of a building on Canal Street.

The battle went on through out the night, and well into the next day before the firefighters were able to hold the fire to the west side of the river. There was a remarkable stand at Adams Street that night, many firefighters were burned by the searing heat and hot cinders that fell upon them and many were over come by the smoke. This heroic fight stopped the fire from traveling north and east into the heart of Chicago's business district. The fire continued to burn to the south jumping over Jackson Street, and was finally stopped at Van Buren Street on the south. An area of over a half mile square was completely consumed by the fire. The chief of the Brigade began shutting down engines, and getting them back in service one at a time, to protect the rest of the city. The firemen had no rest, and very little food for days now. There was a critical shortage of coal to supply the engines. Many hose lines had burst, or were destroyed by the fire, and there was no replacement hose to be had anywhere. After working non stop for over twenty straight hours of tough physical labor, and manning heavy fire hoses the firefighters were thoroughly exhausted.

Our Engine Company 6 was being put back into service, and we all worked in kind of a silence after returning to our house from the fire. The foreman Bill Musham said, "Norm, I am proud of you because you stood your ground even with the velocity of that wind and fire" It was a great compliment from a guy who doesn't say much, but as I looked around at the other firemen working to put this engine back into service, I thought to myself; I'm proud to be a Chicago firefighter. All their faces were black from soot, their hair was singed, and they all worked hard at the Saturday night fire. I have been working as a fireman for some six years now, and I have seen a number of fires, but never like that fire.

Firefighter Joe Lauf was rigging up the harnesses for the horses, and Ed Jennings had just finished getting the furnace on the engine ready for the next fire. As I looked out the doors in front of the fire house you could see the shadow of the sun setting on the side of the house across the street. It was 5:31 pm, and the temperature outside was 79 degrees. A hot dry wind continued to blow out of the southwest. I wish it would rain, I thought to myself as I turned and walked back in the fire house.

John O'Rourke was in the stable in the rear, tending to the horses. It seems that "Spencer", one of the "Morgan's" has some burns on the sides of his legs, and he is also suffering from fatigue. John said if you clean the burns real good, and the area around them and then dry the area, and with a clean cloth and apply some liniment to the burns, they will heal. As I looked around the stable at the rest of the horses, I could see burns on many of them.

The Chief and his Buggy man pull up in front of the fire house, and we all walked up to the front. The Chief told Musham, as he climbed down from the buggy, that many fire companies were out of service from last nights fire. Many of the men are in bad shape. "How are you guys?" he asked Musham. "We're okay. A little tired, but we're in-service,' Musham said. "That's good, because many of the firefighters are being cared for at their homes," the Chief said.

John O'Rourke gets a bucket of water for the Chief's horse, and hands it to his buggyman; because he could tell the horse was hot and dry. As the Chief climbs back up to his buggy, he says,"If you guys get anything hit it as hard as you can."

Bill Musham called all of us together by his desk, and he opened a folder that the Chief gave him. The population of Chicago has grown to 334,270 people, and it is now thirty-six square miles of mostly wooden framed buildings. On October 1, 1871 the Chicago Fire Department had sixteen engine companies, each one had a hose cart, there was 48,000 feet of hose, there were four truck companies, and two hose elevators. "But tonight men," the Captain said, "one quarter of the Chicago Fire Department is crippled because of all the fires in the last week, especially last night's fire. So let's all try to get some rest tonight. Who's got the first watch?" " I do "Capt," said Joe Lauf."Okay, Joe, let's keep a good eye out there." At about 8:30 pm Bill Musham made the entry into the company journal.

Firefighter Joe Lauf climbed up to the top of the tower of Engine 6, and began looking toward the west. The western sky was red and there was a terrible whirlwind that seemed to be increasing. Looking to the east he could almost see Lake Michigan, although it was dark, all was clear. A short distance to the north of Engine 6 was an old residential district of small dwellings, and a few stores on DeKoven Street. There were some people out in that area, but most were getting ready to retire for the evening. The firemen knew the area well by Taylor and De Koven Streets, because of fires in the past.

There was a small parcel of property that belonged to Patrick and Catherine O'Leary, and they had a very respectable milk business. Their house was in the middle of the lot. In the rear of the lot was a barn with milking cows, a small calf, and one horse. There was also a small house that the O'Leary's owned in the front of the lot that was rented to the McLaughlin's. There was a party at McLaughlin's for a visiting brother from Ireland; you could hear the fiddle playing.

At about 9:00 pm a fire was spotted in the O'Leary barn, at 137 DeKoven by a peg-legged man, he began yelling, "Fire, fire!" In the tower of Engine 6 firefighter Joe Lauf now spots the fire north and a little west of the fire house. "Company Still" he said. "It's at about Taylor just west of Clinton Street."

The gong was sounded and Engine 6 went into action, the horses were hitched to the hose cart and the engine, and soon we were out of the fire house. As Engine 6 was racing north on Canal Street, the wind was blowing furiously from the southwest, and there was debris flying every where. The O'Leary house was situated on the North side of De Koven Street, about six lots West of Clinton Street. Upon their arrival on the scene, Captain Musham ordered firefighters Doolan and O'Rouke to lead out a hose line through the small alley way toward the burning barn. Engineer Jennings secured a fire hydrant on DeKoven Street, and it was just a matter of minutes before they had water on this fire. Eye witnesses said that the top of the barn had flames coming out of it, the crowd that gathered thought the fire would be out in a short time.

Captain Musham was helping us with the line, and said, "This is not so bad. We can put this fire out; just keep that line on the fire. I will be right back. Engine 5 should now be on Taylor Street," he said. "They will bring their hose line on the north side of the barn. I began to play the stream of water on the roof of the burning barn, but the wind was breaking up the stream of water. Musham ran back to take a look to see if Engine 5 was there and working. As he made his way out on to DeKoven Street he discovered Engine 5 had not yet arrived. "Where the hell is Engine 5?" he said to himself as he ran toward Taylor Street.

Flames were spreading fast to the adjoining structures just behind the barn, and a large number of people were gathering to the west of the fire. Musham frantically ran back to his men, and yelled to them that the fire was burning out of control. "We need to bring this line around to the Taylor Street side, because we are here by ourselves." O'Rourke said, "Where is Engine 5?"

At 9: 00 pm in the courthouse cupola tower, Mathais Schafer was the watchman, and he sights a fire southwest of the courthouse. Immediately he calls down via-a-voice tube to the operator, William Brown, on the third floor where the Central Fire Alarm Telegraph Office is located.

Schafer told the operator Brown to strike Box 342 which is located on the corner of Canalport Avenue and Halsted Street. This Box is about one mile southwest of the O'Leary's where Engine 6 was desperately trying to stop this fire for over twenty minutes. Now Engine 5 that was responding to the Box realized that the Fire Alarm Office has made a miscalculation. They turn their engine around, and are now racing east on Taylor Street toward Engine 6, and the fire that is burning out of control.

Engine Company 5 has hooked up the fire hydrant and was just beginning to generate steam when something went wrong with the fire box on the engine, and they had to start all over again. Engine 6 was playing their line on four separate fires, but before engine 5 could get their water the fire had jumped over Taylor Street and was heading eastward toward the old planning mill.

Now at about 9:30pm, Shafer, up in the courthouse cupola noticed that the fire was growing and can now see that he has made a mistake about "Box 342". He called back down on the voice tube, and asked Brown to "Strike Box 319" which would be closer to the fire. But, Brown refused to strike that Box because he did not want to confuse the firefighters by striking a different alarm. As a result, there was a big delay in the full response of all remaining fire companies to the scene.

Within thirty minutes Engine Company 6 arrived on the scene at 137 DeKoven Street. There were at least fifteen fires burning on the north side of Taylor Street. The Old Planning Mill was located on the corner of Taylor and Canal Streets, just about one block east of where the fire originated. There were piles and piles of wood shavings as high as a two-story building. When the burning cinders landed all over the dry wood shavings, they literally exploded into flames.

Bill Musham and his men labored hard to stop this fire, but the fire roared out of control. They could see fire over a block away far from the reach of their fire hoses. "Oh my God, please help us tonight," said Musham as he looked to the north east.

A second and a third alarm were turned in by Fire Marshal Robert Williams. But to no avail; even the responding engines that came from a distance knew that this fire was already larger than the fire that they fought last night. Chief Williams knew if we were going to stop this raging fire we must set up a front line of defense, and it has to be at the river.

The fire did not get any farther west than to Jefferson Street, because of that southwest wind that just seemed to increase as the night went on. The fire has divided into two solid columns running north; the smaller one was between Jefferson Street and Clinton Street and the larger one between Canal Street and the rivers edge. From Canal Street east was now a wall of fire, being driven by a violent windstorm. The fire reached right over the south branch of the Chicago River, and ignited a chair factory located on the eastern bank of the river.

The Chicago firefighters fought this battle foot by foot, and sometimes being almost surrounded by fire. The Chief ordered the men to move back to the north where an engine was again connected to a hydrant at Polk and Clinton Streets. With two fire streams working they sent their water in both directions desperately trying to stop this inferno from traveling any farther north, but they were in a bad position in-between the two burning columns of fire.

Chief Williams set up a defense line at the river, and the Van Buren Street Bridge. In a meeting with his Assistant Chiefs Schank, Walters, and Benner, the Chief asked for a progress report. They all said that the fire is now east of the river. John Schank said that some burning material from the cottages on the river had flown some four blocks through the air and has ignited the steeple of St. Paul's Church, and we don't even have an engine company to send over there. Loranz Walter said that the Bateham Lumber Mill on the river bank is now burning and with all that lumber burning we would need four engines just to fight that fire.

Frantically hundreds of people were running west to get over the Van Buren Street Bridge, because of the flying embers, smoke and the fire. The sky above Chicago that night had what many people and firefighters referred as a mass of fire like in a balloon that was just floating in the air.

By this time all of Chicago's firefighters who were able to work were now on duty, and of the sixteen engines there were only twelve that were able to pump. The Chiefs informed the Fire Marshal Williams that all of the equipment they had was mobilized, and there are three separate fires burning out of control. They also told the Fire Marshal that all of the men were desperately fighting the fires, but it looked like nothing could prevent the fires from connecting to one another. The Chief asked, "Can we get in front of the fire? We must save the business district or all of Chicago will be gone forever," John Schank said,"Chief, we will have to divide the fire companies, and give up this west side as lost."

Williams said, "Alright, then take six of the engines over the Madison Street Bridge and get set up at LaSalle and Dearborn Streets." Chief Williams ordered the Truck companies to help evacuate the people over the VanBuren Street Bridge then move into the business district. By this time the fire was north of the VanBuren Bridge all the way to Adams Street, and the VanBuren Bridge was on fire with many people trying to cross. But, the firefighters of Engine 14 set-up their hose lines, and with fire on both ends, the brave firefighters not only fought the fire but assisted hundreds of people to safety, before the bridge collapsed into the river.

Along both banks of the Chicago River, the east side and west side, was a wall of fire almost one mile long, over one-hundred feet in the air, being fanned by sixty-mile an hour wind. "It", the fire, was a perfect engine that had the fuel, the oxygen and the wind to sustain burning continuously until it ran out of fuel. The column of fire moved swiftly north into the old wooden shanties of the poor people in Conley's Patch, and in a matter of minuets, they were all gone - consumed by the fire. High in the sky, flames hurled burning cinders east toward the business district, and the buildings on LaSalle Street. The brave firefighters were throwing streams of water on structures before the fire reached them.

As the wall of flames pushed east, the water that the firemen were wetting down the buildings with instantly turned to vapor, and burst into flames.

At 12:00 midnight Chief Williams told the Mayor of Chicago, Rosewell Mason, that the firefighters have used all the means they had to stop the inferno of flames, and that the Fire Department had to make a firebreak by blowing up some buildings. The Mayor, who was in shock like most of the people in Chicago, told chief Williams to do anything he could to stop this fire. The Mayor then began sending out wires to New York City, Milwaukee, and St. Louis appealing for help and any extra fire fighting equipment that they could spare.

Meanwhile, Chief Williams asked the men under his command to recommend someone to get dynamite, and begin blowing buildings right away. A former Alderman, James Hildreth, began to experiment in the

Union National Bank, but after all the work setting up the dynamite; it only blew out some windows. And while the alderman tried working with the explosives the fire just kept leaping from one building to another. The principal streets in the loop district for dry goods and merchandise were both Lake Street and Randolph Street. The Old Garden City Hotel on Market Street was now burning. The firefighters were exhausted, but they continued the battle even though their fire streams had no effect on the raging inferno around them.

On the river front just north of Market Street, almost everyday you could witness hundreds of vessels anchored, or being towed in from the lake. They were loaded with coal, wood, and all kinds of merchandise from all over the country. But, tonight the boats and all the vessels were now being turned around and were frantically trying to get back out to the lake before they caught on fire from the burning embers that were flying everywhere.

Engine Company 6 was one of the six engines to set up the last front on Madison Street between LaSalle Street and Dearborn Street. After the explosions failed, the weary firefighters began pulling back, as the fire progressed further north and east. The Courthouse tower was now burning, and the fire raged down LaSalle Street instantly igniting the grand hotels of Chicago. I said,"Hey Captain, they let the prisoners out of jail in the courthouse, all the people are now gone. We are trying to put water on this one building, and there are ten other buildings fully ablaze around us."

Musham said, "You're right Norm, and gave the orders to move all the horses and equipment toward Lake Michigan. We can set up a fire line on Michigan Avenue." So once again the tired firefighters moved east toward the Lake, and as they were leading the horses down Washington Street they saw the famous courthouse bell tower fall with a force like they have never heard before. The raging fire had over ten large buildings burning, and it lit up the sky as bright as day. Hot flying cinders continued to rain down on top of everyone and there was nowhere to hide. The firefighters tried to open the hydrant at South Water Street & Michigan Avenue, but there was no water. The Chief rolled up in his buggy, and said, there is no water because the water works was now aflame, and the fire is now unchecked in the North Division.

At this time in the fire some 2000 structures were burning, and people were so frightened they were imagining their worst fears. All you could hear was the crying and screaming as people fled to the only salvation from the heat, LAKE MICHIGAN.

Frightened cattle, sheep, and horses ran together, as they stampeded i herds. Horses hitched to wagons went out far enough in to the water to get relief from the radiant heat. Both man and beast were running into Lake Michigan. The people of Chicago just stood in the water and watched the city as they once knew it disappearing! The fire burned itself out on Monday evening, October 9th at the north end of Lincoln Park at Fullerton Avenue. It was about 10:30 pm and it stopped burning about four miles north of its point of origin, in the O'Leary's barn.

On Tuesday morning Chicago began counting its losses. The fire destroyed over two thousand acres just in the central section of the city. Over seventeen thousand homes burned to the ground, and some ninety thousand people were left homeless. There were over three hundred people dead, and that was only the people accounted for; there were most likely many more!

Chicago was overwhelmed with sorrow and in a catatonic liker state of shock for a while, but not for long. A recovery was in the works, and city offices began a relief program in the first Congregational Church. To stop looting, about five thousand police were appointed with only a white piece of cloth for a Badge. Tents were brought in to supply temporary shelter. The sale of whiskey was against the law!

On the Southeast corner of Adams and LaSalle Streets, a brick structure was constructed and it was now known as the "Old Rookery". This was now the new headquarters of the Chicago Fire Department. There were many injuries of firefighters after the fire, but fortunately there was no loss of life. Sixty of the firefighters who fought the fire lost almost everything they had.

Brother firefighters from all over America and Canada sent relief to Chicago firefighters. Donations came in and totaled $11,480.55. There is no other profession like firefighting, because we all fight the same enemy. If one of cities in the fire service has a loss, then all cities suffer the loss, and support the city that is down. A committee was appointed to distribute the funds for brother firefighter who needed assistance, and it given to them right away.

In time, all the Chicago Fire Departments engines and hook & ladder trucks, hose elevators, and supply wagons were back in service from the fire. Three of them had to be rebuilt. The top chief s placed in command were, Fire Marshal R.A. Williams, First Assistant Marshal, Mathias Benner, Second Assistant, Charles S. Petrie, and Third Assistant Marshal, William H. Musham Musham was the foreman of "Little Giant: Engine 6 our fire

Company and you know they were the first engine to the O'Leary's barn fire.

Mayor Joseph Medill had his way, and got an Act passed that gave him the power over all the paid employees of Chicago. One of Mayor Medill's primary acts as Mayor was to get the politics out of the Chicago Fire Department. Aldermen and heads of committees had been getting jobs for their friends, and they were not even trained to be firefighters. This made Medill mad as hell, because firefighting was such a unique profession, and you must be trained to perform this type of work, effectively and efficiently!

The Chicago Fire Department has gone through many changes, and there are now about 200 men on the job. Engine 6 was assigned a new Foreman, James Enright, who replaced William Musham. Standing out in front of the "Little Giant's" fire house I was talking to O'Rourke about our new foreman, Enright. We both liked him from the first day. He was a down to earth guy with some humor, and he was a good fireman. I was only on the job for eight years, but I had been in some battles that will be always being remembered, throughout history.

John O'Rouke and I had become very close friends, like brothers, since I had joined the fire service. They worked on a busy engine company that was respected throughout the department. The "Little Giant" was always clean and shiny; the horses that pulled the engine were strong and good looking. When they drove down the streets of Chicago people stopped in their tracks to watch them pass.

Our fire house Engine Company 6 was located in the farthest southwest fire house in the city. Day by day Chicago's business district began to grow rapidly. As a matter of fact, Chicago and her people looked this rebuilding project right in the eye, and all they could see was recovery, and how much better Chicago will be this time. Bricks were the rule to rebuild Chicago, and the years after the fire, bricks went for $6.00 per thousand to almost $17.00 per thousand, and the Brick industry began to boom. Everybody that owned land could borrow money, and they did to rebuild their homes. But this time, with bricks not wood. A New Fire Limits ordinance was passed in February 1872; that stated there would be no erection of any wooden structures. But, not everyone obeyed the ordinance; there were a rowdy bunch of people in the south Division that lived in a large tract of mostly wooden buildings.

This area was beginning to cause trouble, because they refused to begin to use bricks on new structures, and would not remove wooden canopies and cornices. On a very warm afternoon about at about 4:00pm I was up in the watch tower of Engine 6, looking out at the new city that was building up right in front of me. As I was looking, I spied smoke, and began yelling down to the first floor of the two story wooden framed firehouse. "We got a hit. Fire, Fire!" I yelled.

North and to the east, smoke was rising over the river at about Clark & Polk Streets. The fire was in the south district where all the wooden structures were located. By the time we got water on this fire there were six buildings totally engulfed in flames. While this fire was burning out of control, a meeting was taking place at headquarters.

Mayor Medill was arguing with the police and fire commissioners about who would control the fire department. "Politics, it's always politics, politics!" O'Rouke shouted. "They are in there, and we are out here fighting the fire, and they are arguing about our fate!" The fire burned for almost twelve hours. Exhausted from heat and smoke, the firefighters barely had the last of the fire out, and another fire broke out in the North Division. Smoke was seen around Milwaukee and Sangamon Streets and again the firefighters battled another large fire in Chiacago. Twenty-five to thirty structures were lost in the north division, and between fifteen and twenty in the south division. There was an insurance loss of over four million dollars.

Now the politicians are paying attention, and they got another meeting together, but this time it's a special meeting on July 15, 1874. While the North Division fire was still burning, rules were proposed about who will run the Chicago Fire Department, and those rules were adopted unanimously. These were those new rules.

1. The fire department would be reorganized
2. Absolute authority was vested in the hands of the fire marshal;
3. Fire limits were to be rigidly enforced,
4. Regulations put in place against frame structures;
5. City water main would be enlarged;
6. Combustibles in the city were prohibited, and
7. All wood awnings, cornices and cupolas were to be torn down.

Fire Marshal Benner agreed to cooperate with the Chicago Board of Underwriters with reorganizing of the fire department. General William Shalers of the United States Army was hired. His job was to get the fire department in shape by training the firemen like Army trained its soldiers by drilling and instructing.

General Shaler's process to reorganize the fire department was to make one Brigade under the command of the Fire Marshal as Chief Officer. The department would be divided into six battalions; each battalion was assigned an Assistant Fire Marshal, who would be the Chief of that Battalion. Each Battalion had a boundary, that was comprised of several fire Companies. The Rank of Company Foreman was eliminated and the new rank of Captain replaced this rank in the fire company. Also eliminated was the Assistant Foreman; this rank was now Lieutenant. Instead of privates like in the Army, the fire department now had firemen. .

This finally ended this political control of the department's bullshit, and the end of the Police and Fire Commissioners. This Board never knew what the needs of the Chicago Fire Department were, and they didn't care. It was a matter of historical record, that at the time of the great Chicago Fire the Chicago Fire Department was in bad shape. There were many injuries to firefighters and damaged fire hoses from fires that should have been replaced the week before the Great Chicago Fire.

The fire that occurred at 209 South Canal Street, on Saturday, October 7, 1871 would have been the Great Chicago Fire if it had not been for the heroic acts of Chicago Firemen that night.

As the years went on, a new program of building began, and that brought in a wave of immigrants into Chicago from everywhere. Barges began bringing in stone, sand, and bricks via the Illinois & Michigan Canal. Most of the rubble from the Chicago fire was now taken over to Lake Michigan, south of the river, and pushed in to make new real estate. Small businesses started springing up everywhere. In less than three and half years, three quarters of the burned out area of what was Chicago, was now back up, but now in bricks and stone, not wood!

It seemed like every night there was a big fire along the Chicago River, so the city of Chicago and the fire department employed a tug boat, and then equipped it with fire appliances, and large nozzles. Firemen were detailed from the department to man the new tug boat.

"I sure hope I don't get detailed to the boat, because I get sea sick." Norm said. Captain Enright said, "I know one thing boys, it might be a lot of work pulling all that hose to get from the fire to the boat, but once you have water from the boat you can put out a lot of fire, with a 1 ½ inch nozzle."

"Well they won't be replacing the engines, or our grand horses that pull these Rigs, I hope," O'Rourke said. "How many horses do we have on the job now Cap? O'Rourke asked.

"Well, last count I think there are three hundred and sixty-six, plus what they have in reserve at the farm on Archer & Western," said Captain Enright.

Sitting around the wood burning stove drinking coffee, the Captain was talking about the house work, and things that needed to be done that morning. Norm said, "Hey Capt., how does the city pick out the horses to pull an engine that weighs 7000 pounds?"

"Well, first of all, the horse needs to be sized like a Morgan or a Percheron. They are about 16 hh or 17 hh which means they are measured in hands and inches. A man's hand is about four inches, so the horse is sixty eight inches or 17 hh or hands. A work horse must weigh in at between 1200 to 1400 pounds. The horse must be good tempered, and it has to be a good worker, no slackers, like some firemen I know." Enright stood up and said, "Enough of this bullshit, let's get this place cleaned up. It is winter time, and there is a lot of work that needs to be done before any meal times are assigned."

Just as we started the house work, in the front door came their chief, Chief Murphy. Everyone liked to work with him, and he had a special liking for me because I made him laugh with my sayings and jokes! Chief Murphy was excited about a new system that was going to be installed in fourteen engine houses.

"The Chief Operator, John Barrett, in the Fire Alarm Office perfected that system, and you guys are one of the chosen engine companies", the chief said.

"Here is how the system will work. There will be a new electro mechanical device called a "Register" that will be located on a wooden shelf called a "Joker Stand ". These registers will print a series of dashes on paper tape that will indicate numbers that you will use to look up the address of the fire. This new system will allow the department the ability to alert the box alarm signals to all fire houses at the same time that they are receiving it at the Fire Alarm Office." "Also," Chief Murphy said, "a talking circuit phone will be installed on the Joker Stand called the "Talker" The Talker will connect the engine house with the Fire Alarm Office.

Each fire company will be assigned a "Signature"; a number of the engine that could be tapped out on the sounder key. The Fire Alarm Office will call the closest company to a fire location on the sounder key, and then the fire house will answer with their signature followed by the location of the fire that will be given to the engine company on the talker phone. When the fire is over, the engine company will sound their return on the sounder key, and this will tell the Fire Alarm Office they were back in service and ready for another fire call.

"But," I asked, how the hell do we learn all the numbers?" "The department is changing, Norm, and we all will learn," the chief said as he walked out the front doors into the cold winter day.

Captain Enright said we can all look this over after the house work was done. He said by the way, I have Lieutenant Schrrenberg working in for me tonight, because it's my wife's birthday.

John O'Rourke opened the stable doors and gave a whistle to his horse, "Come-on buddy let's go for a walk" as he and Mike Burns, he driver, took hold of the five horses and led them out in front onto Maxwell Street."Let's get them stalls ready Norm, its cold outside," John yelled. "Hey easy on the whip I am only a hired horse," Norm said back with a laugh.

A new kid was assigned to Engine 6, Jimmy Conway, and I told him you clean out the old shit from the stalls, and we will get the new straw and some fresh pine shavings to put down. He looked at me, and wanted to say something, but before he did I just said, 'Get some time on the job kid," and kept going. New straw and pine shavings were laid down in each stall and the door and window was opened to the stable, this was the best way to disinfect the stable. Once the horses were led back in they were watered first before they are fed, this is a rule. The reason we water first is because horses by nature are slow eaters, and require from fifteen and twenty minutes to eat a pound of hay, and about five to ten minutes to eat a pound of grain.

While we clean the rest of the fire house, Captain Enright and engineer Jennings check out the engine. Especially in this cold weather, all the moving parts should be thoroughly oiled, so when we are out on the street in the snow it will not affect the moving parts of the rig.

The meals were assigned, and O'Rourke and I were getting a late dinner. When we walked into Rusty's Grill, there were a few guys sitting on the other side yelling back and forth about something.

When the waitress came over to get our order, I asked her what going on over there? 'Norm,' she said, 'they are bitching about working hours. The unions want to propose that a man works eight hours, instead of working until they're told that the day was over." "Well that's a good idea," I said, "but good luck telling the boss.

O'Rourke says I will take the roast beef, potatoes, and vegetables. "Same here," I said, "and how about some hot bead and coffee too." "Coming right up boys," said the waitress.

"Norm," John said, "I heard that the Mayor was in favor of the eight hour work day, but most of the business men were totally against it. You know what the Golden Rule is don't you? Those who have the gold rule and they will never let the eight hour day happen'

"But, the workers, they have no rights, none at all," I said, "the railroad men, factory workers, and all those that work in the Stock Yards, and that is bullshit! They do what they are told or you're fired!"

They finished eating dinner and began walking back to the fire house. The snow began to fall again, and it was cold outside. "Looks to be about three inches Norm,"John said as the fire house came into view.

The fire house was warm with both wood burning stoves almost glowing; Captain Enright's relief, Lieutenant John Scharrenberg came in to work for him. "He is a great fireman," O'Rourke said, "and he loves to play cards."

We played cards until about 10:00 pm and the Lieutenant asked, "who had first watch" "I do Lu," said the driver of the engine, Mike Burns, and the Lieutenant entered Burn's name in the company journal, and went up to bed. John O'Rourke and I went into the back to give the horses their last watering, and John said "Hey Norm, my wife asked me to invite you, Nancy, and the kids for Turkey dinner on Thanksgiving. "Sure, thanks, I'll asked Nancy. Hey by the way when is thanksgiving?" Norm said. "I think it is next Thursday," John said as he began climbing the stairs, "I'm taken it in" goodnight.

So I walked up to the front of the fire house and looked out the small window in the front doors. It was still snowing out, and the wind was blowing out of the northwest. Just to look at it gave me the shivers. Boy, I sure hope we don't go anywhere tonight I thought to myself, as I began climbing the stairs to the bunk room.

When I entered into the dark bunk room, I found my bunk and sat down and pulled off my big heavy boots. The bunk room is dark, and cold. The only noise that can be heard is engineer Jennings, he snores like the engine. I think I fell asleep and got a wink or two.

Suddenly, the electric current was sent from the Fire Alarm Office to start the register and the bell began to sound strokes in a quick startling succession. The firefighters spring from their beds almost simultaneously with the bell, as if they were lying awake waiting for the fire call. As they came down the stairs all that could be heard was a scurry of feet, and the rush of the fire horses to their post in front of the engine and hose wagon. Mike Burns yelled out the address, the harnesses were tightened. Each man had a specific job to do in order to get these rigs out the door, and to the fire. "That's our fire," Lieutenant Scharrenberg yelled, "Get the led out of your asses. I think that's the Marshall Field Building on State & Washington. "Okay," Burns yelled, "the teams are ready. Get the doors open, get the doors open," he yelled as the big doors swung in. The hose wagon started out onto Maxwell Street into the new fresh snow, followed closely by the steam engine with smoke now beginning to belch out the stack.

At first the horses were a little shocked by the snow, but horses are by nature high strung and very reactive. The driver, Mike Burns takes hold of the reins, stands up and yells "get-up. get-up, gee ayah," and pulls the reins to the left as they turn onto Canal Street. He keeps screaming, "Come-on get it going," as the horses are pulling with all their might, straining their collars, and now are beginning to get footing. The Lieutenant says, "Take the whip, that will get them going,." "No, no we never whip my horses; we're doing just fine, "as they continue into a full gallop. It is a long run to State & Washington Streets, but when engine Company 6 arrives on the scene there is a heavy smoke and fire condition. Fire is noted issuing from the windows on the second floor on the east side of the three-story burning structure.

Chief Murphy ordered Lieutenant Scharrenberg, and the men of engine 6 to lead our hose line up the front stairway to the second floor. As the hose is stretched up the stairs, John O'Rourke takes the line forward down the hallway toward the rear of the burning structure. With Lieutenant Scharrenberg as his heal man; the second firemen on the hose line, while I helped engineer Jennings make the hydrant on State Street.

The fire is generating a lot of smoke from plain cotton, paper, and wood. The hot gases rise upward to the ceiling and begin to bank downward in the long hallway. O'Rourke can now see the red and yellow glow through the smoke at the end of the hallway. I made my way up to where O'Rourke and the Lieutenant are holding the 2 ½ inch hose line

Lieutenant Scharrenberg yells back, "Can we get the truck to ventilate the rear so we can advance this line?" We are down on all fours crawling forward, and it's getting awful hot. Finally we see fire just in front of us, O'Rourke stops and sets up on one knee and hits the fire straight on until it darkens. We push on one foot at time in the hot dark hallway. Just then Engine Company17 advances their line up next to us; I said "Yeah now we have some water power," as we began to move the two hose lines forward.

But, now we are crawling on our bellies, and the ceiling is thick with heavy black smoke with a red and orange glow. Scharrenberg yells "It's over our heads; we can feel the heat on our backs." The firefighters roll over on their backs, pointing the nozzles at the fire over their heads, I began helping Charles Dudley of Engine 17 with his hose line directing it on the ceiling.

The fire darkens a little, but then all of the sudden the blistering heat and smoke came down on us like nothing I have ever felt before. Frantically we try to retreat, and the fire flashed all around us. I began choking and coughing until I lost coconscious.

The lifeless bodies of the four firefighters in that hallway were pulled out by the truck men, and the other firemen that were up in that inferno. They were taken down to State Street. Chief Murphy and the other firemen tried to help them, but to no avail, as they lay in the snow on State Street with steam still emanating from their fire clothes.

Pipeman John O'Rourke and Pipeman Charles Dudley were dead, and Lieutenant Scharrenberg and Pipeman Norman Doolan were breathing, but just barely. Chief Murphy ordered the firefighters to get some warm blankets on Scharrenberg and Doolan, and get them the hell out off the street and into a warm place right away. The fire raged on through out the early morning, and was finally extinguished many hours later.

On December 17, 1877 a little more than a month after the fire Lieutenant Scharrenberg died as a result of smoke inhalation and burns from the Marshall Fields Fire. Pipeman Norman Doolan was taken to his home, and remained in critical condition. Needless to say now Thanksgiving that year was gloomy because the deaths still lingered with all Chicago Firefighters.

Over the next four months I began to feel a lot better, and wanted to get back on the job. Although the doctors disagreed; they said that I had permanent damage to my respiratory system. But, I was not about to listen to a bunch of doctors, because I had a grand idea. I went over to talk to Chief Murphy, and said; if I was to be your "Buggy man" the doctors will let me back on the job, because I won't go into any more fires. "Yeah right," said Murphy; "I will talk to some people and see what I can do." In a matter of days, I was assigned to the 5th Battalion as a "buggyman".

Battalion 5 was located in Truck Company 2's quarters, at 540 West Washington, on the western edge of Chicago's down town business district. The Buggy was pulled by one horse, a "Hackney", and he was about 14 hh. They called him Dutch. In the very early morning hours I was introduced to Dutch because one of the firemen of Truck 2 informed me that this horse has a very spirited temperament. Once in the stable Dutch spied me right away. I looked at the horse as they back him out of his stall; and I thought to myself, this is the horse that will be pulling the buggy I am driving.

There was no movement from the horse when I extended my left hand, but when I held out the right hand, my fist was closed, and when I slowly opened my hand there was a cube of sugar. "Come here, Dutch," I said with a smooth voice. Slowly the horse walked toward me inhaling the scent of the sugar. He quickly licked up the sugar cube, and ever so gently he rubbed his head against my forearm, and from that day on we did well together.

Chief Murphy was always busy doing something, and today was no different. "Get the buggy ready, Norm," he said. "We have some things to do today." It seems that Captain David Kenyon, the Captain of Engine Company 21 invented a fire pole, and this morning all the Chiefs were to be there for the test of his new invention.

He jumped into the seat next to me, and said, "We're going to Engine 21, and I think we are late, so let's get going" I yelled, "Come on Dutch, get up boy." In no time at all, we were in a fast trot towards Roosevelt Road. Chief Murphy told me that Captain Kenyon's new fire pole was a 25-foot piece of pine that the firemen of Engine Company 25 sanded, varnished, and rubbed down with paraffin wax.

The corners were rounded on this new fire pole.

The Chief said to Norm, "I think this pole is a good idea." "Well," I said, "it might be a good idea, but I not going to slide down any pole, and break my neck".

When they arrived at Engine 21, all the big shots were already there, Chief Fire Marshal Benner, Assistant Chief Denis Swenie, and a few others fire companies. The pole was already erected from the bunk room on the second floor, through the flooring and down to the engine floor. No one seemed interested in sliding slide down this new invention. So firefighter George Reid a young black fireman of engine 21, said "get out of the way, I will slide the pole". He walked up to the pole, grabbed on, wrapped his legs around it and with ease slid down to the engine floor.

Well they all enjoyed watching each other slide down the pole. Soon after, Chief Benner ordered fire poles to be installed in all fire houses, because engine Company 21 was using the pole and they were arriving at fires much quicker than any other company.

In April of 1879, after a long, dawn out election, Chicago got a new Mayor, Carter H. Harrison. The new Mayor found out that the city of Chicago was almost broke, and millions of dollars in debt. His first unpopular official order was to have all departments reduce their budgets by twenty-five percent.

Chief Fire Marshal Benner strongly opposed the reduction. "You mean all the other departments?" he said to the Mayor, "but not the Chicago Fire Department!" He was ultimately asked for his resignation the next day, and Denis Swenie became the new Chief Fire Marshal of the Chicago Fire Department. Following his appointment, the fire department lost 41 men, and was now down to three hundred and fifty-five men. Also following Denis Swenie's appointment, all the salaries of fire department were again reduced by five Percent. To top that, by December of 1880 the force had seven battalions. How could more battalions be added when manpower was cut?

I was furious with the city. Firemen were risking their lives every day, living away from their families for days, but the city kept sticking it up our asses. And then, if you get hurt, they give you peanuts to live on.

"So, I know," I told some of the boys in the stable in the back of the firehouse while I was giving Dutch water, "One day you think this was a real good job, but this one platoon system is not easy. Not by a long shot boys; not by a long shot," I said as I walked out of the stable.

By 1886 workers were sick and tired of being told that they can go home when the job's finished. All they wanted was to work for eight hours, for eight hours pay, and then go home to their family. What's wrong with that? The people were uniting on this eight hour day all over Chicago, so they called a rally. The rally began at about 8:30 pm at an open market place called "Haymarket Square", located at DesPlaines just north of Randolph Street which is the western edge of the loop. All they had was a makeshift stage in a wagon for the speakers. Mayor Carter Harrison joined the crowed, but he only stayed for a little while. The rally went on until about 10:00pm, and was drawing to a close when Inspector John Bonfield led one hundred seventy-six police officers in to disperse the crowd.

Just then a bomb exploded, and in all the confusion shots rang out. One police officer was killed by the bomb, six officers died later, and sixty others were injured. The court held that inflammatory speeches were given, and publications were handed out to incite the actions of the mob. Seven of the eight men arrested were given the death sentence, and eight others were given fifteen years in prison. The businessmen of Chicago used this occasion to attack their enemies. The strong arm was once again brought down, and directed the Chicago Police to arrest eight innocent men who organized the rally. Then the businessmen directed the prosecutors, juries, and judges to give out the harshest punishments. The rest of the nation looked on in horror, and disgust as the "kangaroo" court gave out the sentences.

Being back to work was good for me, and being the "Buggyman" for Chief Murphy was the best job for an "Old Timer", as the young firemen now called me. I don't see myself as an old timer at forty-six years old, but

I have has seen a lot. Living in Chicago did not get any better for the next few years, and especially for the injured firefighters. The Firemen's Relief Fund reported that they did not have enough money in the fund to pay the firemen or the families of firemen who were injured or killed in the line of duty. I was telling Chief Murphy about the fund, when the Chief said, "Norm, I know you have been gone from the job for awhile. But while you were recovering from your injuries there was a Revenue Commission appointed in the legislature to work at devising laws to place taxation on corporations, and others to make reasonable contributions to the general welfare of Police Officers and Firemen's pensions," I said, "I did not know that, and I sure hope that Commission is successful."

Chief Murphy said, "I know that things are bad on the department, and throughout Chicago. I did hear some scuttle butt the other day, and if it is true a lot of things will change for the city of Chicago." " Well are you going to tell me what you heard, or do I have to guess?" I said to Chief Murphy. What I heard was that Chicago is in the bidding process for the World's Fair, and if they can bring this World's Fair to Chicago, there will be work for everyone. For the fire department, it would mean bringing back all those firemen that they let go, and the fair itself would need a battalion of new fire companies. I said, "Well that does sound good.

Several months later, the 5th Battalion was traveling north on Dearborn Street while returning from a warehouse fire located just southeast of the loop at14th and Wabash Avenue, Chief Murphy spied some smoke to the west and a little North of their position. "Norm," the Chief said, "there is some smoke out to the West, turn on Washington."

With that I took hold of the reins, and yelled to Dutch Getty – up boy, and I turned the buggy west down Washington Street."I can see it now; it's on the other side of the River, at about Randolph Street," I said as the buggy raced over the Chicago River. With skilled handling to control this fast temperament of a horse, I slowed him down to turn onto Jefferson Street. A large column of smoke was rising up into the blue sky, as I pulled the buggy off to the side of the burning building. People are outside the three-story wood framed building yelling,

The Chief started to put on his fire gear on when we heard someone screaming, Chief Murphy told me to request a 2-11 alarm from the fire alarm box at the corner. The Chief heads toward the burning building, and into the gang way along the south side of the structure, he can hear screaming, "Help us, help us, please help-us: Chief Murphy yelled to firefighters of Truck Company 2 to get ladders up to the south side of the building.

Chief Murphy forced open a door in the rear, and climbed the stairs to the second floor. There was heavy smoke in the hallway, and he could hear children yelling and crying. Chief Murphy started down the hall, the smoke was heavy and he began to crouch down still on his feet feeling the walls. It was getting hotter and the smoke level was almost to the floor, so he is now down on his knees, and then down on his belly moving inward. Finally, a door on his right. He pushed it open, and there in the corner of the room was a mother and four children. The smoke in the room was not as heavy as in the hallway, but opening the door, quickly filled the room with smoke. Chief Murphy told the mother to take the big boy with her as he took the infant and a small child under his coat and grabbed the last kid. He told the mother to take hold of the back of his coat so they could go out. He told her not to let go, no matter what. Out into the hallway, Chief Murphy led the mother and her children down on their knees choking and coughing toward the rear. Then the smoke was a little lighter, and they could hear the voices of the other firefighters who took hold of the mother and her 2 older children out of harms' way. Chief Murphy continued down the rear stairs until he was outside, and came around the front where he took the baby and the infant out from under his coat and handed them to a woman in the street.

Firemen were leading hose lines up the front stairs; Chief Murphy began giving orders to the Captain of the truck to get the roof open. There was a heavy smoke and fire condition, with fire now issuing out the windows of the very room where the children were. Two hose lines were hitting the fire from the outside where the heavy fire was issuing

"All right guys, when that fire is knocked down get in there and wash it down," said chief Murphy. I was just staring at Chief Murphy, after he just made this heroic rescue; he began fighting the fire without saying anything. In all my years on this job that was one of the most heroic deeds I had ever seen. The fire was extinguished and the engines began shutting down their hose lines, and again the firemen begin to roll up their hose, and began getting the engine back in service for the next fire.

A Metal Fund was created through donations of Lambert Tree, and Sir Carter Harrison. On March 4, 1887 in the presence of hundreds of people, Mayor Harrison presented Edward W. Murphy, Chief of the 5th Battalion, with the very first Lambert Tree Award for the rescue of that mother and her children.

The World's Fair is the talk of the town, more and more news was coming out everyday about the World's Fair and the people of Chicago were getting very excited. A resolution was passed by an interstate exposition committee in preparation for a Columbian World's Fair. In 1889 the American movement became very intense with a fierce rivalry developing among leading cities that wished to host the World's Fair. Washington and St Louis were very important contenders, but the real fierce struggle was between New York City and Chicago. It was during this time that Chicago received its name "The Windy City", not because of the physical blasts of wind from Lake Michigan, but because of all the "Hot Air" from the boosters that were plugging away for Chicago. Most people thought that Chicago could not deliver all the promises that they were making. Negotiations in Washington were far enough advanced for an exposition "bill" to be introduced by Senator Cullom of Illinois to the Senate.

The hard fought contest between Chicago and New York was finally decided in the House of Representatives giving Chicago the win on the eighth ballot. It was told that on the last day an outstanding banker named Lyman Gage raised several million dollars for Chicago, and this gave Chicago the edge over New York.

The Chicago people involved with the World's Fair were of course prominent businessmen. At a fancy dinner party at Mr. Ferdinand Peck's thirty room mansion located at 1826 South Michigan Avenue, many well known citizens of the 1890's were in attendance. Ferdinand Peck was offered the presidency of the World's Fair, but Peck declined in favor of Harlow Niles Higinbotham, a director of Marshall Field and Company. Peck would serve as First Vice President and Chairman of the Finance Committee. Planning of the Fair was crucial, but not as crucial as the money needed. Another five million dollar bond had to be floated. In order to float this bond it was necessary to get state approval in Springfield. It was at this time, the Fair was given the official name. THE WORLD'S COLUMBIAN EXPOSITION.

Fireman Norm Doolan is the "buggyman" of the 5th Battalion, and he knows each and everyone of the Firemen, Captain's Lieutenant's and Engineer's in the battalion, and many other Chief's. When some one wanted to know what was going on, they would ask Norm, and if he didn't know what you were looking for, he would bull shit his way through it, and make it sound believable.

The 5th Battalion had been very busy in 1890, with a record number of fires calls in the month of March. In the back of the fire house I began talking about Firefighter John Michels, on Engine Company 30, who was working at a 2- 11 Alarm fire yesterday, and died in the street at Divisic and Ashland.

The Chiefs had a meeting this morning; one of the Chiefs was talking about the fire that occurred yesterday. Firefighter Michels was working on the second floor with his hose line, the smoke was bad, but not that bad, Michels asked for a break on the line and right at that time he started to have chest pains. He called out to one of the guys, and fell to the floor. They carried him down, but by the time they got him down to the street, he was dead. He died as a direct result of various physical ill effects that were associated with long-term smoke inhalation. Firefighters are in this shit smoke day after day, and this exposure to smoke can eventually cause a fireman a heart attack!

One of the Truck men, Firefighter David Burke, asked me about some kind of benefits for Michel's family. There was in place a Beneficiary Act for the widows. It would never bring back Firefighter Michels, but it will give some financial relief to his wife and children. They will become beneficiaries of the fund immediately. Michel's wife would receive $30.00 per month, if she stays a widow, and the children would receive $ 6.00 per month until each child reaches the age of sixteen years old.

"Hey Norm, what do you know about the World's Fair?" Burke asked. "Well," I said, "there are questions like, where will it be held? What would it look like? Who would build it? These questions were being asked by many people. "But me personally, I think it's grand about our city hosting the fair. It will do a lot for Chicago. Jobs will be available and money will be made," I said. Chief Murphy walks to the back, and said to Norm, "Is the "buggy ready yet? Norm said, "Hey boss, easy on the whip I'm only a hired horse. "Ha-Ha"

In the summer of 1890 a guy named Frederick Olmsted was hired as the landscape architect for laying out the grounds for the Fair. Daniel Burnham and John Root were hired as the chief architects of the buildings. On a large brown piece of paper in the early planning, John Root drew the main essentials of the lagoons and canals within the Jackson Park location, where the Fair was placed.

Burnham assigned construction of the buildings to a number of architects for expediency and uniform appearances of the buildings. There was no time to sit around, working began right away. This committee began traveling from the east to west, meetings and gathering day-in and day-out, trying to bring in the best architects in the business to Chicago so work could begin quickly. Work did come to Chicago like I told the firemen it would; work like we have never seen before. Every type of trades' men you can think of had come to work on the World's Fair. The architects put the buildings where they wanted, but there needed to be input from the Chicago Fire Department; that was an order from the Mayor himself!

A meeting was set up with the architects of the Fair, Burnham & Root, and the Chicago Fire Department, Chief Fire Marshal Denis Swenie and Assistant Chief Fire Marshal John Campion. There was a large print of the Fair layout that was affixed to the wall in Burnham's office. Swenie just gave a look at Campion, "This is big, real big," he said. After sitting down at the table questions were asked like; where would the most strategic places to have fire stations; what type of apparatus should there be on the grounds of this Fair, and most important; how and where would the alarm system should be installed. "The Fair grounds are going to be hard to cover, because of the projected size, so we will need at least six fire stations," said Chief Swenie. "If not, more," remarked Chief Campion.

"How about the water system for hydrants?" Chief Campion asked. "You know boys we are on a very strict budget, "said Burnham, "and also remember, the Fair will only be here for six months." Burnham gave Chief Swenie a set of the prints of the grounds where the Fair would be built."See what you can do with these, and we will meet next week." said Burnham.

The next day Chiefs Swenie and Campion met and went over the prints and decided where to put the fire stations, the alarm system and pull stations, what type of apparatus would be needed. A new battalion would have to be organized, and Chief Fire Marshal Swenie already knew who he wanted as the Chief of the new 14th Battalion, Chief Murphy, and of course his buggyman, Firefighter Norm Doolan! Chief Campion concurred.

The Jackson Park site where the Fair was being built was about seven miles south of the Chicago loop on seven hundred acres of land right on Lake Michigan. The Fair grounds were much larger than they appeared on the print. The boundaries were from 55th Street on the North end and 67th Street on the South end. Lake Michigan was the Eastern border extending west to Stony Island Avenue. On the west border of Stony Island Avenue there was a stretch of land that is called the Midway Plaisance that went from 59th Street to 60th Street from Stony Island to Cottage Grove. This was an area of about one mile.

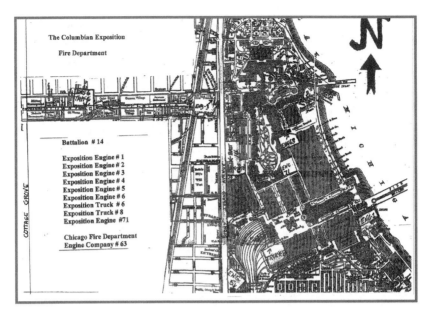

The Exposition had already organized an auxiliary fire department while the construction was going on but, they knew in a very short period of time that they would need the expertise of the Chicago Fire Department. These men from the auxiliary fire department would have to be trained in firefighting. "How will we accomplish that without having any actual fires?" asked Chief Murphy.

Chief Swenie said, "We have decided that the 14th Battalion Headquarters will be located in the service building at 62nd and Stony Island. It is centrally located and the Columbian Guard has one engine company there already. It looks like whatever we ask for from Burnham is going to be argued, because of the cost. He always uses the excuse that the Fair is only going to be here for six months. I stepped up and said, "How about all the Chicago firefighters that were going to be hired back that were let go, what happened to that?'

"There will be trains, carriages, horses, and boats, bringing in thousands of people to this fair, we will need an army of trained firefighters to keep them safe. Nothing against this Colombian Guard, but these guys are not trained to rescue people." I said to all the Chiefs.

"You are right Norm," Chief Campion said, "but every time we ask for anything we get shot down with, there is not enough money to pay for firefighters." I said, "This committee is so cheap; they wouldn't give flies to a blind spider." They all just laughed, and started working on what can be done.

Chiefs Swenie, Campion, and Murphy went to work, figuring out what was needed, and after hours of planning the decision was made. There will be five engine companies and two truck companies, all supported by the Columbian Guards. Each company will have a Chicago Fire Department officer, and one firefighter. The Chicago Fire Department Engine 63 will be placed in the center of the Fair at the north end of the Manufactures building. All personal on Engine 63 are Chicago Firefighters. Total manpower will not be more than one hundred men, and they will be called The Colombian Fire Brigade.

There will be one hundred sixty- one fire alarm boxes installed on the fair grounds and they will be connected to the city telegraph system and terminated at the Englewood Fire Alarm Office. As for the hydrants, the mains will be on the outside streets; 55th, 67th and Stony Island.

There are mains running into the grounds, but they are not high pressure. So, to reach the large structures a "Fire Boat" is being purchased. The boat is a light draught made special for the lagoon. She will be docked in the lagoon next to the Electricity building, and will be manned by Chicago firefighters. "All right, men," said Chief Swenie, "That's it, so let's get to work and put this new battalion together." "Hey Chief," I said, "What do we call the new fire boat? "The boat will be Engine Company 71 and she will be called the "Fire Queen, "the Chief said.

Chief Murphy and I arrived at their new headquarters at 62nd and Stony Island. Doolan says this isn't a firehouse, it's an oversized garage. The building is the service building of the Columbian Exposition; it is a two-story wooden framed structure about 200 feet long. The fire department only took a small portion at one end of the building with Engine 2 and the 14th battalion. I introduced myself and the Chief to the men of the Columbian Guard, as they are called. They escorted me to the stable where Dutch had his own stall and the Chief had his own quarters upstairs above the engine.

Everyday was drill, drill, drill and more drill, until the Columbian Guard learned how to fight fires, lead out hose, and climb ladders. As opening day of the Fair was approaching, Chief Murphy was holding class at one of the largest structures of the Fair, the Manufactures building, that measured out 1,687' x 787'. Generally these buildings are mainly constructed of iron and timber similar to how a train depot is constructed, but filled with wooden partitions. The exterior, or the outer surface of the building, is constructed of wood and a lightweight durable mixture of plaster, cement and jute fibers. A building this size is dangerous when on fire, I thought to myself. They looked at every building one by one, some times with the fire companies, but most of the time just Chief Murphy and me. After looking at all sides of a building, Chief Murphy would make some notes about possible problems. If there was a fire or some other incident at some particular building how would the fire department get inside these massive structures to attack the situation?

In the afternoon Norm, the Chief would stay over at Engine Company 63"s fire house. The Chief liked it for good reasons. The Captain of engine 63 was one of Chief Murphy's old buddies, James Fitzpatrick. They worked on Engine 5 in the city together for years as firefighters. Chief Murphy handpicked Captain Fitzpatrick with the approval of Chief Fire Marshal Swenie. Fitzpatrick was one of the best engine Captains on the fire department, and ran a no-nonsense company. Every Chicago Firefighter that was detailed to the "World's Fair" was hand-picked or recommended. The Fire Stations were to be placed in the following order:

The Columbian Exposition Fire Department:

Engine Company 1 was set up just off the Casino Pier at Lake Michigan on the East side of the Agricultural Building. The Chicago Fire Department Captain was James Garvey.

Engine Company 2 was set up set up at the Service Building at 62nd and Stony Island along with the 14th Battalion. The officer of engine 2 was Lieutenant John Meyers

Engine Company 3 was set up by the northwest gate at 59th and Stony Island. The Chicago Fire Department Captain was Burton Page.

Engine Company 4 was set up at the north entrance gate on 56th street. The Chicago Fire Department Captain was Charles Purves.

Engine Company 5 was set up just inside the south gate. The Chicago Fire Department officer was Lieutenant John Pyne.

Engine Company 6 and Truck Company 6 were set up on the Midway Plaisance, by the Ferris Wheel about five blocks east of the Cottage Grove west entrance. Chicago Fire Department Michael Ehret was the Captain of Engine 6, and Lieutenant Joseph Ballak was the officer of Truck 6.

Truck Company 8 was set up on the south side of the Railway Terminal Station. Both Truck Companies6 and 8 had Chemical Engines.

Engine 71 "The Fire Queen" was in the lagoon on the north side of the Electricity Building. The Chicago Fire Queen Captain, was Thomas Barry.

In no time, I knew each and every one of the firefighters by name, and would start out most conversations by saying "What's up Punk". I also knew the guy at the west entrance on Cottage Grove Avenue. So if any Chicago Firefighter or Officer wanted to bring their family in to the Fair, all they would do is get a hold of me. Each day I would drop the Chief off at Engine Company 6 that was located by the Ferris Wheel on The Midway Plaisance. Then "Dutch' would trot over to the Cottage Grove gate, and I would leave the names of the firefighters that were going to attend the Fair that particular day. The guy at the Cottage Grove gate was Tony, and he had relatives working all over the Fair. His brother was one of the head guy's at the Cold Storage Building. You can get anything there, it was the greatest refrigerator on Earth!

As the Chief and I made the rounds from house to house, we had just left engine 4, and Lieutenant Purves said, "Chief, take a look at the walls of these buildings. They are all white with some type of paint." Traveling South, just to their left was the Art Galleries Building, and they were applying white paint to the West side of the building. Chief Murphy told me to pull over to the Art Galleries Building. I pulled the reins to the left and "Dutch "turned the buggy into the lawn in front of the massive building. Chief Murphy walked up the lawn where he met a worker who was the foreman. "What type of coating are they applying to the walls?" asked Chief Murphy.

The foreman told him that all the buildings were to be painted with this "Polychromatic Treatment" This white paint was being applied by compressed air gun."They're going to call the Fair The White City," he said, as he returned to the side of the building to join the rest of his crew.

The Chief said, "What do you think of that paint? I think it smells like its oil based and it will burn like all hell."Well, guess what, they're painting all the buildings white. They better hurry with that stuff, because opening day is not very far away," I said, as the buggy pulls away from the side of the Art Galleries Building.

Back at Engine 63 firehouse, the Chief and Captain Fitzpatrick are talking about the paint. Chief Murphy said all the buildings are going to be painted white, and they are calling the Fair The White City. Captain Fitzpatrick said the outer surface of most of the large buildings is a wood veneer with the outer coating being a mixture of plaster, cement and jute, with white paint as a top coating.

"It just seems that the whole thing is a facade or something not real, but, hey, what do we know. We're just firemen, right "Boss?" said Fitzpatrick. Engine 63's house was more like Chicago Fire house; all the firefighters were Chicago guys. Not that anything was wrong with the "Columbian Guard Firefighters"; it's just Chicago firemen were close to one another because of the job. Engine 63 was located in about the center of the Fair, so most of the Chief's time was spent there. He liked to know what was happening with the rest of the fire department so he could listen to the fire calls that occurred in the city. The fire house was located on the north side of the Manufacturer's Building, the largest of all the buildings at the Fair. It could hold 100,000 people. "Oh boy, how could our fire engine, with so few men do anything if something happened to a building with that many people inside of it, Fitz?" said Chief Murphy.

"Well, Norm," Chief Murphy said to me, "get the buggy, let's go see the greatest refrigerator in the world, the Cold Storage Building. There is a meeting there about a thimble that is to be placed on top of this chimney and I have to be there. A thimble is a device that deflects sparks and heat at the top of a chimney." The buggy rode south behind the giant buildings and around the south end of the Lagoon. "It's like a different world here compared to working in the city." the Chief said to Norm as Dutch pulled them around the Transportation Terminal. Up along the west side fence that backs up to Stony Island Avenue was this big oblong building, the Cold Storage Building.

It seems to be constructed in the same material as the other buildings. Chief Murphy pulls out the blueprint of the Cold Storage Building. This building is 130' x 255'six stories high to the roof line. "Another monster," the Chief said."Look at those towers in the corners," said Norm, "They have to be ten stories high." The Chief looked down at the drawing, one hundred and fifteen feet to be exact, but look at that thing in the center of the structure. It matches the corner towers, but it is almost two hundred feet from the ground. The sheet shows that there is a cast iron smoke stack connected to three boilers in the structure. This chimney from the base up to the roof is sixty feet, and from the roof to the top is another one hundred forty-nine feet to the thimble on the very tip!

I tied Dutch in front, and told the guy to watch him, but don't touch him, because he bites! We went through the front doors of the Cold Storage Building. There were workers everywhere. We were met by the construction foreman. He informed the Chief that an insulated brick lining was being installed around the cast iron chimney, and a spiral stairway was being built around leading all the way to the very top."Boy," I said, "that's a hell of a stairway. Who is the carpenter?" "There is only one guy that could build a stairway like this," said the foreman. "That is John Newquest, the greatest stair builder around. He is involved with many projects around the fair. Would you like to meet him Chief? He's up at the top, but I can get him." Chief Murphy said "No, no. It's okay. We will be back at a later time." "This Cold Storage Building is not being built along with the other buildings of the Fair," the foreman said; "this building is being built by an independent builder, Hercules Iron Works. This company owned by a different Burnham brother, Franklin Burnham." Very interesting Chief Murphy thought to himself.

There was roll call every morning at 08:00 hours and uniforms were inspected by Chief Murphy. He would tell us that soon the world will be looking at us. When they go back to wherever they came from, I want them to have a good opinion of the Chicago Fire Department. Every morning after roll call, the men would be drilled on the alarm system by me, because I was the best at the Box system at the Fair, and in the city. "Pay close attention to any Box that rings in (9 s), I said, "because all the Boxes inside the Fairgrounds begin with the number (9). Our Boxes are number 9113 thru 9634. When you respond, remember your going to a building number, not an address. So learn your building numbers. Chief Murphy knew his men, and they knew what he expected of them when an incident occurs.

As opening day approaches the final construction jobs were finished. Many small things were not completed, but the work would go on night and day right up to opening day. The Columbian Exposition Fire Brigade had been drilled and they were ready. They all looked grand in their very distinctive uniforms of the Colombian Guard, and also the Chicago Fire Department members who all wore their badges on there uniforms at all times. In front of the Service Building all members went through a very stringent inspection by the Chief Fire Marshal Swenie, and Assistant Fire Marshal Campion.

Opening Day finally came, May 1, 1893 and people filed in by the hundreds. At about 8:00 pm the President of the United States, Grover Cleveland, gave a very supportive speech in front of the Administration Building. With thousands of people watching he then pushed the "Button" turning on all the electrical lights. It was a site to see! Chief Murphy had his fingers crossed hoping that nothing would go wrong, and nothing did, thank God!

Opening Day came and went, people were everywhere enjoying themselves. Adult admission to the Fairgrounds was fifty cents, very high for the times, but surely worth the money once you entered. Kids under twelve years old could get in for twenty-five cents. The Fair became an Architectural show mostly because of the "White City" thing; the principal marvel of the Exposition was its architecture. There were sculptures every where. They were brought in from all over the world, and there were flags flying high from all the buildings.

The crowds in the grand plaza in front of the Administration Building were very large, and also across the bridges people numbered in the thousands. That sent shivers up Chief Murphy's back on a hot day in June. "We are but a small band of men," the Chief said to me and Captain Fitzpatrick," sitting in the shade of a tree in front of Engine 63's quarters. "If anything big occurred here, we could be absorbed by this crowd. I just can't imagine what would happen," the Chief said.

It was a lot harder to get around with the buggy among all these people. Most of the time we are stopped by people admiring Dutch's Bay Brown color with his markings of white on his head and legs. People would stop us in our tracks to admire Dutch. Upon our arrival at Engine 6's firehouse there was a line of people four deep in the front apron of the firehouse. Chief Murphy jumped out of the buggy and ran inside the station to tell Captain Ehret to clear the people away from in front. "Why in the hell are they there, anyway?" the Chief asked. "Oh, Chief, that's the line for the Ferris Wheel." "Well, if you got a run with them in front of the station it would slow you down, so get them across the street now."

The Captain called the Columbian Guard to the front, and the crowd was moved over to the other side of the street. Dutch and I ran up to the Cottage Grove entrance to see Tony. "Any firemen today?" I asked. "About twenty," he said. I turned the buggy and said, "Thanks Tony, see you tomorrow."

Chief Murphy finished up his rounds, and we headed back to Engine 63 quarters. I took Dutch in the back stable to water him down. The boys were talking about how nifty it was that there were thousands of people at the Fair today. I said, "It is real hard to maneuver the buggy in this crowd. I can't imagine trying to get an engine through the crowds. So, if you guys get a run, make a lot of noise, to clear the way." Around the 3:00 pm mid afternoon hour, Chief Murphy walked up to me and asked, "How many days since opening day?" "Well, Chief today is June 17TH so I think it is the forty-seventh day." "Why," asked Norm."Well," Chief Murphy said, "a very good friend of mine is coming to the Fair today, and I want to meet him later. Will you get the buggy ready Norm? I have some paper work to prepare for Captain Garvey at Engine 1's house over at the Casino Pier,' the Chief said.

I hitched Dutch up in a matter of minuets, the Chief climbed up, and we were on our way. Around the Manufacture Building I noticed that engine1 was hitching up their team in a hurry. As we approached the station the Chief yelled to Captain Jim Garvey, "Where are you going? It's Box 9134, The Cold Storage Building," Chief Garvey answered. Chief Murphy looked to the West, and there was smoke at the top of the chimney. "Let's go," I said to Dutch as he turned the buggy toward the fire, and we raced off.

Upon their arrival on the scene, Engine 63 was already on the scene with Truck Company 8. Captain Fitzpatrick took one look up the 200 foot tower and said, "Get that hose wagon over to this doorway." Fitzpatrick went inside the building and found the spiral stairway in the center of this building and returned to the door. Captain Fitzpatrick ordered the firefighters to the door; and told each man to take a fifty foot length of hose, get it over your shoulders and follow me.

As they climbed up, and up the stairway to the roof they were about sixty feet from the ground. They quickly regrouped and started up the rest of the stairs that went around the chimney. By the time Captain Fitzpatrick finally arrived at the top, he was exhausted. They came out onto a colonnade or balcony that was about twenty feet below the actual top of the chimney that was burning, and they are about 180 feet above the ground.

The Captain tied off the rope and climbed the last of the stairs where he could see fire at the very tip of the of the wooden ornamental top. He called down to get the rest of that hose up there, and to tell them "to send the water". The message echoed down the stairway and out to the engine, and the engineer who already had a good head of steam, opened the valve, "Here's your Water" the Engineer said. Within a minute the air whooshed from the 1 1/8 inch Nozzle on the top of the stairway, followed by a blast of water, and within ten minutes there were two hose lines on this fire. That is when Captain Fitzpatrick saw the top of the chimney, which was about one foot below the wooden ornamental top. The firefighters concentrated their streams on the burning wooden top, soon the fire was extinguished.

Picking up all the hose was hard work, and they took their time, but it was nothing like hauling the hose up the stairs... As the firefighters began coming down the spiral stairway they could see that the brick work was not completed around the cast iron chiminey, they only bricked it up to a little above the roof level.

Captain Fitzpatrick called for Chief Murphy to come up to the top of the tower. Together they examined the burned area, noting that the chimney stack was lower than the wooden elements at the top. Also the brick that insulates the wooden stairway around the chimney was not completed all the way to the top; this has Chief Murphy very concerned.

An emergency meeting was called with the committee and Chiefs Swenie, Campion, and Murphy. Chief Murphy told the committee and the Chiefs of the hazards that they encountered in the Cold Storage Building. Burnham told the fire department this concession was not built by the Fair; it was constructed by an independent contractor. The representative from that company stated that the thimble that is to be installed was not installed and delivery was delayed. The thimble was expected to arrive soon and would then be installed on the top of the chimney. Oh, and please tell the firemen that they sure did a good job putting out the fire, said Harlow Higinbotham, the President of the Exposition. "But, that is your job, isn't it Chief? Putting out fires!" as he walked out of the room.

"I did not like that snide remark from that guy, Higinbotham,' Chief Murphy said to me. We made our rounds, and Chief Murphy congratulated all the firefighters on a job well done in the Cold Storage building, he told them that were the most perfect lead – out of hose, that he has ever seen.

He took his officers Lieutenant Purves, Captain Burton Page, Captain James Garvey and Captain James Fitzpatrick to the side and told them what great coordination they had. "That was what is called our best work," Chief Murphy told his men.

The Forth of July was just celebration after celebration. Many firefighters and their families were at the Fair enjoying the fireworks displays. Most people did not make too much of the fire in the Cold Storage Building, and the only thing that was said, was about the great effort of the Columbian Exposition fire department in extinguishing the fire.

The Chief had to meet with some friends, they stayed together for a while and had a magnificent time. "Looking out at the Basin, and the Court of Honor could just take your breath way,' Murphy's friend said. "Truly magnificent, the size of the buildings, the Statue of the Republic that stands almost 75 feet in the air, it's a great day in Chicago,' Chief Murphy said.

But, everyone's first pick for the number one all around attraction at the Fair was the Ferris Wheel, because at its full height it was two hundred sixty-four feet. The view from the top was remarkable. You could see most of Chicago and the entire Fair. There were thirty-six wooden veneered cars on the Ferris Wheel and sixty people could fit into each car. I thought to myself, we have been here for four months; it doesn't look that magnificent to me any more.

As the hot days of the summer are here we try to get the rounds completed early before it gets too hot outside. It is going to be a high of 88 degrees today. Every time we pass by that smoke stack on the Cold Storage Building, the Chief looks up and just shakes his head. "To think that with all the money here at the Fair," the Chief said, "one would think that a thimble, that could save the building from burning down, would be on the top of the to-do list."

Engine Company 4 was our last stop of our rounds; Lieutenant Purves always had something to say to the Chief about the manpower or the equipment. I would go in the back and talk to the boys. But what I want to do is to get back to Engine 63, and take a little rest before we have to go to some doings this afternoon. Chief Murphy climbed back up in the buggy. We were finally finished with all the paperwork. "The shade under that tree sounds good now," the Chief said, as we were traveled south.

It was just before the noon hour when Chief Murphy spied some smoke from that chimney in the Cold Storage Building. "There is smoke coming from the chimney," he said, "There is always smoke coming from that chimney," I said "Back to him." Let's get over there." Just then we saw Engine 63 come barreling around the corner toward the Cold Storage Building. We could not see very well until we came around the Transportation Building, but there was a heavy smoke condition at the top of the Cupola again, "God damm it" Murphy said. Fitzpatrick said to the men, "We have another fire. Looks like the same as the last one; let's get that hose wagon right here by the door." Each man will take a fifty-foot horseshoe over their shoulder, and we will start up.

Chief Murphy sent me around to the rear of the building. The chief was always looking and he sees flames now issuing from the top the building. He went to the pull station box 9134 and requests a 2-11 alarm. With a 2-11 alarm, the Englewood Fire Alarm Office will send four more engine companies, one truck company, and another Battalion Chief to the fire.

As Captain Fitzpatrick yells, "Come on boys, let's see if we can knock this one out like we did the last time", as they ascended up the spiral stairway.

"Let's all pull the hose boys, pull, and keep pulling." As they got up to the roof level, the firefighters were huffing and puffing. "Don't move, rest right there for a minute," Captain Fitzpatrick said to his lead men. He yelled down the stairs, "Get some more hose up here." "I got it, Fitz," said Lieutenant Purves, as he climbed on to the roof. "You keep going up with those three guys."

Captain Fitzpatrick took the three firefighters up the spiral stairway, another one hundred ten feet over the roof to the balcony of the tower. The firefighters straightened out the hose on the floor of the balcony and Captain Fitzpatrick gave the order to send the water. The brave firefighters began going up the small spiral stairway that led up to the burning cupola. Captain Jim Garvey told Captain Fitz that he would take the pipe or the nozzle up to the top this time. The smoke was blowing down onto the stairway and Fitzpatrick said it wasn't this bad the last time. Finally when they got to the top, the fire was larger than the last time. They were hitting the fire and the smoke began getting heavy. The next thing, the stairs were burning at the very top.

"We have to back down," Garvey yelled. There were now about twenty firefighters up in the tower balcony. There was a lot of smoke as Captain Garvey backed down the stairway. Just then Captain Burton began yelling to Lieutenant Purves and Captain Fitzpatrick, "There is heavy heat and smoke that is coming up the stairs from down below," he yelled.

Captain Fitzpatrick looked over the side of the balcony and saw firefighters on the roof below waving their arms frantically. He then saw heavy smoke billowing out of the tower below them. They took the hose and began shooting the water down the stairs. They now knew that fire was below them. Just then the water in the hose was cut off by the fire below. There was a rope tied up to the rail of the balcony and one firefighter began to slide down, then another. The rope was now burning and both men were burned and suffered injuries as they fell to the roof below. The hose was tied off the rail and again the firefighters began to slide down, but fell to their deaths. Within a minute they were cut off from escape. Frantically the firefighters ran from one side of the balcony to the other, in a hope that a way to safety might be found.

The interior of the tower was on fire, and there was heavy smoke under a lot of pressure coming out of a hole in the side of the tower, about twenty feet above the roof Chief Murphy requested a 3-11 alarm; four more engine companies, and one truck company responded to the alarm. The firefighters below knew the true conditions of what was happening, and were powerless to save their brothers who were so far up in the tower. An attempt was made to fight the fire on the floors below inside the building, but the heat and smoke drove the firefighters back out of the burning building. There was an upward draft from below that caused the fire to spread with fury throughout the building and up the spiral stairway. There was no escape, except by jumping from the tower to the main roof below. Everyone that was watching from below was in disbelief! When they saw the first firefighter jump, a man yelled, "Oh my God!"

I ran up the stairway leading to the tower to see if I could help rescue anyone from the roof. But, one by one they started to jump, right before the eyes of a horrified crowd of thousands of people that had gathered outside of the burning Cold Storage Building. There are no words that could describe the sounds of the bodies as they hit the roof.

Several of the men that jumped went right through the flimsy roof. Suddenly there was a movement in the tower, and it began to list to one side. The next man that jumped from the burning tower was Captain James Fitzpatrick. His body came down so hard that he actually stuck in the roof. I ran out onto the roof with another firefighter, picked up the body of Captain Fitzpatrick and lowered him by rope to the ground. He was then taken to the emergency hospital with internal injuries and a fractured leg; he died a short time later.

There were two small explosions of gases that occurred, and now fire was throughout the top floor of the structure, and they cleared off the roof. Chief Swenie was on the scene, and requested Two Special Alarms bringing a total of twenty engines to the fire. Then the burning tower came crashing down, and the structure began to burn fiercely because the structure was constructed of mostly pine wood and plaster. There were also barrels of oil on the first floor. The fire burned intensely for hours before they could start to begin to recover the bodies of their brother firefighters.

In the end, twelve men had jumped to their deaths, four members of the Chicago Fire Department, eight Columbian Exposition Firefighters, and three civilians. Five men were injured and were taken to the hospital. The thousands of eyewitnesses of this horrible catastrophe screamed out loud, many turned away, and some fainted when the tower and building collapsed to the ground.

President Higinbotham sat at his big desk in his short sleeve shirt, saying very little about the calamity at the Cold Storage Building. The World's Fair stables, just north of the Cold Storage Building, caught fire and the fire extended to the roofs of several hotels across Stony Island Avenue. With twenty-six engines and five truck companies working on all the structures that were burning, the firefighters had their hands full.

They were able to save the hotels, but the stables burned to the ground along with the Cold Storage Building. In less than two hours from the start of the fire the whole building was almost level to the ground."I cannot believe what has happened," I said to Chief Murphy.

As the fires were extinguished, fire companies were being put back into service. One by one, as fast as they could fire engines were put back in service in their respective fire districts that were unprotected.

By late evening, many loved ones of the firefighters anxiously waited to find out the news of their missing husbands, fathers, and brothers. Throughout the night firefighters continued to work their engine streams on the ruins of the Cold Storage Building.

In the early morning of Tuesday July 11, 1893, as the sun rose over Lake Michigan, the ruins of what was left of the Cold Storage Building were still smoldering. There was a mountain about fifteen feet high of debris that would have to be sifted through in order to find and recover the charred bodies of the brave men. The search was slow and tedious because of the amount of iron, steel bars, and machinery. With the aid of heavy machinery to lift up the network of pipes from the cooling system, the firefighters dug deeper in the ruins of charred timbers for the missing men. It was miserable work digging; but not one of us left the scene. The heavy crane would pull away the bucket with a load of debris, and a dozen off duty Chicago Firefighters would climb back in over the rubble. Down on their knees they dug through the wet ashes, and still hot smoldering timbers. They knew that the men were near the smoke stack, or chimney, because that is where these brave men were seen jumping from the tower.

The digging and searching went on for three days after the fire originated, and the work never stopped until all of the remains of all the bodies were recovered and taken to the World's Fair Morgue. This fire claimed the lives of fifteen men three Chicago Fire Department Captains and one Lieutenant, eight Columbian Guard Firefighters, two Cold Storage workers, and one electrician.

Four days after the fire the newspapers began to tell how the fifteen brave men died, the newspaper found out about the construction errors. They also found out that the insurance company cancelled the fire insurance on the Cold Storage Building after the first fire. Questions began to arise about who was to be responsible for this tragic event.

Chief Murphy and firemen knew how mad Captain Fitzpatrick was about the incomplete construction of the "Thimble", on top of the chimney. The Fair went on, but it seemed that all those who attended knew of the fire. Before the building was even reduced to ashes, a man named Byron Smith who was attending the Fair and witnessed the terrible event, started a relief fund for the families of the fallen heroes. In just a matter of minutes several thousand dollars were raised. The money was paid to President Higinbotham's office.

Chicago suffered a loss of its finest, was the headlines in the Chicago newspapers. I began making the rounds too many firehouses, asking the firemen to get their uniforms on to perform a very grim duty. The firefighters assembled in front of the church and slowly, with all the grace they had, the pallbears removed the caskets from the horse drawn hearses. In the back of the church a solo singer sang "Amazing Grace" as each casket was placed in the front of the church. Hundreds of mourners filed past the flag draped caskets of the brave men. Eulogies were given for each fallen and thanks were given to the people for coming out and honoring their loved ones. You could feel the warmth and true concern for the widows and orphans. The brother of Captain Fitzpatrick said the families would like to thank each and everyone who contributed to the Fund that was started at the Fair grounds, and continues to grow. The men were buried at Oakwood Cemetery, and the honor guard stood at attention as each casket was lowered into the ground.

The following morning a meeting was held at the Administration Building on the Fair grounds. In attendance was Mayor Carter Harrison, the building committee for the Exposition, and several architects. Attending from the Chicago Fire Department was Fire Marshal Swenie, Assistant Fire Marshal Campion and Battalion Chief Murphy. The meeting began with Chief Swenie stating, almost before they sat down, that after the first fire at the Cold Storage Building, Chief Murphy informed you, pointing his finger at this committee, of the dangers on top of that structure.

Basically, what he told you was that the unfinished chimney with the wood cupola built over the top of the chimney was extremely dangerous. Then this committee said that a "Thimble" was to be placed on top of the chimney, and that would eliminate the hazard.

"It was never installed!" Swenie exclaimed in a very loud voice. His anger and utter frustration were showing through. Again Harlow Higinbotham said that the structure was not built by the Exposition contractors. It was constructed by private contractors. He said, "You will have to take it up with them." Chief Murphy lunged across the table and grabbed Higinbotham by his tie and said, "Listen you lousy little bastard. Fifteen men are dead, and this committee could have prevented their deaths from happening, but you did not!" Chiefs Swenie and Campion restrained Chief Murphy before he hit him, and they forced him back in to his seat.

The Architect, Franklin Burnham, stood up at the table and said, "I am the one who designed the Cold Storage Building and drew up the plans. If this job was carried out like I designed it, this fire would never have occurred in the first place. Chief John Campion pushed back his chair and stood up and said, "The fire department deals with accidents every day, and this was not an accident. People knew about this and did nothing to fix it. I have looked around this room, and I don't see that son of a bitch who was the Manager of the Hercules Iron Works Company here. This guy was warned about the thimble that was not installed on top of that chimney by several people including myself," said Chief Campion. The Manager's reply to the Chief at the time he was warned about failing to install the thimble, was "There were just too many important things to occupy my time and, installing the thimble wasn't one of them. "Today," said Chief Campion, "I would like to have him tell that to widows; I would like him to tell the orphaned children of those brave firemen, that arrogant son of a bitch!"

Standing in the back of the room was Mr. Sullivan an Architect, who had been a critic of the Cold Storage Building, and the half assed construction errors in all the buildings at the Fair. Sullivan continued by saying that was the reason why the insurance was cancelled right after the first fire." Didn't that tell you something?" as he pointed his finger at Franklin Burnham. Franklin Burnham answered in a hushed voice; "I didn't know that the insurance was cancelled."

Higinbotham and the rest of the committee knew by now that these fire department officials were pissed off! And no matter what was said, it was not going to satisfy them. The subject of bravery was brought up. John Mitchell, one of the committee members said, not a one of the brave firefighters died without honor. The meeting calmed down and words were now spoken of the families that have been left behind. They talked about the Fund that was started, and how it had grown to several thousand dollars. A decision was made that Sunday July 23, 1893; the gate receipts for the Fair would be given up to the Fund.

Chief Swenie looked over at Chief Murphy, and gave him a nod! It was unanimous to everyone at the meeting that contributions would be given either to Mayor Harrison or to Harlow Higinbotham. The Fund would be deposited with the Illinois Trust and Savings Bank, and each case of the injured or of the dead would be investigated. If a family was in distress, immediate payment was to be made to help them. The remainder of the money was to be invested for the orphan's education.

No words can describe the gloom of this awful catastrophe. So the following minutes were adopted and signed by all who were in attendance.

The Exposition mourns beneath the shadow of a dreadful sacrifice, strong and brave men obedient to the call of duty, and fearless of danger, without flinching, faced death before our eyes. While we deprecate the waste of noble lives, we recognize the steadfastness of true heroes, shown as well by the living as by the dead. To the living we offer honor and sorrow. The mourning friends and stricken relatives, burdened with anguish at their sudden, cruel and irreparable loss, we commend with tenderest sympathy, to the care of the loving Father of all bereaved souls, when merciful kindness is their ultimate solace and their sure protection.

After Chief Murphy told me about the meeting, what was said, who said what, and the deal that was made, and I just put my head down and said, "More political bullshit". Not one of these sons of bitches will admit that they were responsible for the loss of all these men. Although there were some nice words in the minutes, it's just doesn't do it for me, I want out of this place," I said.

Chief Murphy and Fireman Norman Doolan were transferred back to the 5th Battalion, their old battalion in Truck Company 2's quarters, and they never returned to the World's Fair again. The injured firefighters from the Cold Storage fire would lie in the hospital for months, with broken bones, smoke inhalation, and burns that were disfiguring, and just too terrible to think about.

The relief fund continued to grow to over one hundred thousand dollars, and it will not stop there as Chicago was continuing to respond to the needs of the Fund. As the Fair continued there were many profits from performances that were donated to the Fund for the benefit of the brave men. On Saturday October 28, 1893, three days before the end of the World's Fair, a person who was dissatisfied with existing conditions in Chicago, shot and killed the popular Mayor of Chicago" Carter Harrison in" the doorway of his home.

When the World's Fair came to an end, it was disclosed that about twenty seven million people attended the Fair. It cost about thirty million to build and run the Fair, and the total receipts at the gates added up to about thirty-three million dollars, four million in concessions, which made possible a ten percent dividend to the stockholders!

In late December Chief Murphy and I were returning to our firehouse on Washington Street, just west of Chicago's business district, when out of the corner of my eye I spied a woman with three small children standing on the corner. She appeared to be crying. As they approached I said, "Hey, Chief, isn't that Billy Dennings wife, one of the firefighters who were killed at the Cold Storage fire?" As the buggy pulled up to them, I jumped down and introduced myself. "Yes, I remember you from the funeral for my husband," the woman said. I asked if there was something wrong, and why was she crying. Mrs. Dennings said that she had just come out of the Illinois Trust and Savings Bank, where she had attempted to withdraw some money from the Fund, but was refused. Chief Murphy got down, and asked her,

"How much have you withdrawn so far?" "Nothing," she said, "Nothing, I am broke. I don't have food and I can't pay my rent,."

I picked up the kids and put them in the back of the buggy "Come on over to the firehouse, it's warm and we can look into this for you" I said Back at the firehouse Chief Murphy called over to truck Company 3, and talked to Patrick McElligot, the Lieutenant. His wife is best friends with Captain Fitzpatricks wife. Chief asked the Lieutenant if he could find out from Mrs. Fitzpatrick how to withdraw money from the Fund. It was found out that not one of the widows had received any money from the Fund, and that none of the widows were even contacted by the committee. Now, I was mad as hell. I went to the Illinois Trust Bank and asked to talk to someone about the Fund. The women said if you leave your name I will have someone contact you, I explained to the women in the bank about the Fund. She said I know my husband and I made a donation, I told her about Mrs. Dennings, and if she could find out how much money is now in the Fund, it would be a big help. She told me that she could get in trouble for this, but walked away and when she returned she handed me a piece of paper and said goodbye. Outside the bank, I opened up the piece of paper, and saw the amount of the Fund.$104,138.02

I met Chief Murphy at the firehouse, and told him how much money was in the Widow and Orphan's Fund. Chief Murphy said that he would inform Chiefs Swenie and Campion and let them know about how much money was in the Fund. I informed Chief Murphy that I was going to talk to Mrs. Purves, the widow of Lieutenant Charles Purves, and see if she received any money from the fund.

Lieutenant Purves' widow told me she has not received any money, nor was she contacted by anyone about the Fund. She also said that she and her sister were cleaning stairs and lobbies, because they have no money. With tears in her eyes she told me, my kids have holes in their shoes and it is winter time. She asked, "Why hasn't Mr. Higinbotham sent out a letter or a statement telling us what is going to happen with this Fund. Since Charles has died the only money I have received was from the city it was only twenty two dollars."

I was pissed off, so I went to meet with Captain Fitzpatrick's brother, Mike. He is a Chicago Police Officer, and he was also very pissed off. Mike Fitzpatrick told me, " I can get a couple of guys and we will find out what is going on with this guy Higinbotham. If I find out that he is trying to cheat these widows out of even a dime, I will break his fucking legs."

I told Chief Murphy about Captain Fitzpatrick's brother, and how mad he was about what was going on with the Fund. "Well, don't do anything," the Chief said, "because after I told Chief Swenie he too became a little suspicious of what is going on. He informed me that an investigation will be started by the corporation counsel, and that is the way it will be handled". I said, "All right, but I am going to do a little investigating myself."

Officer Mike Fitzpatrick has a lawyer friend, his name is John Ambrose and his father was a Chief on the Chicago Fire Department, and you know how he feels about this mess. Along with two of the widow's of the Cold Storage fire, they all paid a visit to Mister Harlow Higinbotham's office at the bank. Harlow Higinbotham was very upset that these people came to his bank and demanded to talk with him about the Fund.

Officer Fitzpatrick introduced himself to Mr. Higinbotham, and told him that they heard that the Fund for the fallen firefighters was over one hundred thousand dollars, but the widows and orphans have never seen one dollar of this money. He also informed Mr. Higinbotham that none of the other recipients have even met with you, about how the money was to be distributed. Mr. Higinbotham admitted that he never met with any of the widows or orphans of the firefighters that were killed in the fire at the Cold Storage Building, because there was no reason to do so. Mr. Higinbotham continued to tell them that this Fund was intended as an endowment, and that the widows were never to get any money or a settlement from it, only from the interest that the Fund accrued.

Captain Fitzpatrick's brother Mike stepped up to Higinbotham's desk and said, "Listen, my brother gave his life to this city." He continued by saying, "this Fund was started by the people of Chicago for the "Immediate Relief" of the suffering widows and orphans. So far as can be learned, not a one of them has received any relief, immediate or otherwise. We want to know how much money is in the Fund. We also know that money is being received almost daily, but there has been no word from you or anyone else on the committee as to how this money will be distributed to the widows."

The attorney now stepped up; "My name is John Ambrose I will be working on behalf of the widows and orphans. I am going to get in touch with the corporation counsel of Chicago, and we are going to need to know each and everyone that is on this committee with you." Harlow Higinbotham looked up at John Ambrose, and said, "That is none of your business who is on this committee." "Well, that's where you are wrong, Mr. Higinbotham, because I am representing the widows of the fallen hero's pro-bon-no; I will get a court order." "Get out of my office!" Higinbotham began to scream. His assistant came in and held the door open as they left.

In the mean time the word has gone out throughout the fire department that the Fund money was not being given to the widows and orphans to whom it was meant for. On my own I found out the men who are on the committee with Higinbotham who were entrusted to manage the Fund. I also found out that Bernard Sunny not only was on the Fund committee, but he was also present at the meeting after the Cold Storage Building fire. He is Higinbotham''s first mate and I found out where he worked.

One night after the New Year of 1894, I picked some very special firemen namely Henry Bassett, and Bill Mayer. These two were especially upset with the fact that some one could cheat the widows and orphans out of this money. When Mr. Bernard Sunny was leaving his work, we followed him to his home at 18th and Prairie Avenue just to the south of Chicago's business district. Just as Mr. Sunny began to climb his front stairs to his home, the boys walked up to him. It was dark outside. At first he was startled, and then said, "Can I help you?" and I said, "Yeah you sure can, are you on the committee of the Cold Storage Fund?" Sunny said, "why and who's asking?" Henry Bassett stepped up and said, "I am asking, because my brother was killed in the Cold Storage fire, and he left a wife and three kids, and they are starving. The question I have for you Mr. Sunny," Henry said, "Is why hasn't any money from the Fund been released?" Then I asked Mr. Sunny if he knew that an investigation was underway by the corporation counsel.

"Well," Mr. Sunny said, "I really don't know too much about the Fund, because Mr. Higinbotham has been in charge of it so far." "Well how many meetings has there been concerning the Cold Storage Fund?" Henry asked. "None that I know of," replied Sunny. "Well, get in touch with your friend Harlow, and tell him that we mean business! We want that money to be released to the widows and orphans. Also tell him that the next time we meet maybe a couple of broken bones will move things along," Henry said.

Mr. Sunny ran up the stairs to his house, and as he opened the door I yelled to him. "Oh Bern", or do you like being called Bernard? Also, tell Higinbotham that we know where he lives, and Mitchell, Wilson, and Upham, and we are going to the Chicago Tribune if we don't hear from him tomorrow."

That same evening after dinner, Mr. Sunny met with Harlow Higinbotham and told him about the three men that met him at his home. "Who were they?" asked Higginbotham. "I don't know, but I think they were firemen, and they told me that if the money was not distributed to the widows and orphans soon, that they will be back, and they will break my bones! They also said to tell you, Harlow that they know where you live, and Mitchell, Wilson, and Upham, I am, afraid," said Bernard Sunny.

'They can't tell me what to do, they are just a bunch of thugs who try and use scare tactics," said Higinbotham. "Well, I don't know if you think that the corporation counsel of Chicago are a bunch of thugs, because an investigation is being started to find out what has been done with the Cold Storage Fund money," said Sunny. "Oh, and by the way, the three thugs also said, soon the Chicago Tribune will know about the story.

The very next morning at the bank of Mr. Harlow Higinbotham, four handsome firemen dressed in their uniforms walked into the bank. They were Battalion Chief James Horan, Chief Murphy, Lieutenant Dennis Doyle, and me," Storming Norman Doolan", the guy that just won't quit until this money is given to the widows of the fallen firefighters. Harlow Higinbotham went right into his office with his assistant as soon as he saw the firefighters enter the bank. Soon after the assistant came out and addressed the group, by saying, "Mr. Higinbotham is very busy today, and does not have time to see any of you people today." Chief Horan walked right by the assistant, and opened the door to Higinbotham's office. Mr. Higinbotham stood up and said, "Didn't my assistant tell you that I don't have time for you today?" . In a very loud voice Big Jim Horan said, "Make time Mr. Banker. We have a few questions to ask you," as the rest of the firemen walked into the office.

"Do you know why we're here Mr. Higinbotham?" said Chief Horan."No, I don't, and I am a very busy man," said Harlow Higinbotham. "We are here because we have all contributed to the Fund for our fallen brothers who courageously died at the fire in the Cold Storage Building at the World's Fair. Do you remember the fire Mr. Banker?" said Horan. "Yes I do!" "We want to know where our hard earned money went to, Mr. Banker, since it has not gone to those to whom we gave it". There was silence! "Also, we need to know how much money is presently in the Fund," asked Horan.

"That is none of your business," said Higinbotham."It is only the committees business," he said with a heavy voice."Well that's where you are wrong again, Mr. Banker," Horan said, "Because my Mother does not have a lot of money, but gave her savings to the widows and orphans of those men. I am sure that you would be better off talking to me, than to my Mother, because she sent me, NOT the fire department. Do I make myself clear Mr. Banker?" asked Chief Horan as he slammed his big fist down on Higinbotham's desk

"As a matter of fact, I think the committee has a meeting scheduled for today," said Higinbotham, "and I will have an answerer to your questions by Monday." Lieutenant Dennis Doyle stepped up, and said, "No you won't, you will have an answer tomorrow, because we are coming back with a Tribune reporter in the morning" I don't ever think that I felt so proud to be a firefighter, as I did that very morning in Higinbotham's office. If he even blinks wrong we will stomp him, and he knows it!

The committee came to an agreement the next day, and not to Higinbotham's liking. Each one of the Widow's will receive two thousand dollars, and the remainder of the Fund money will be invested for the Orphans in a trust. Each one of the women was brought in, and signed an agreement of the terms. This money will not bring back their husbands or fathers but it will change their financial lives forever.

The World's Fair was over for all of Chicago, but not for the fire department. The abandoned and vacant buildings were sold off to a Chicago wrecking and salvage company. The work of taking down the structures would be a monumental task, with many man-hours expended. But, on January 8, 1894 a blaze broke out in the vacant Casino at the southeast corner of the Court of Honor! This fire took down the Casino, the music hall, and part of the Manufacturers building before firemen were able to stop it in the sub-zero weather. It took sixteen hours to control and extinguish the 3-11 alarm blaze. This fire was bad luck for the firemen, but it was good luck for the wrecking company, because now they won't need to take down those buildings; the firefighters did it for them!

Again in the last week of February 1894, another, accidentally on purpose fire occurred, this time the fire took down two more of those giant buildings; the agriculture and the machinery buildings. Again, bad luck for the Chicago Fire Department, but good luck for the wrecking company. Again on July 5, 1894 the most spectacular of all the accidentally on purpose fires, took down the terminal station, the mines building, and last but not least, the gigantic manufacturers building. The firefighters poured water on the ruins for some five days.

By the summer's end, the only structure still standing was the well built Fine Arts Building that later became the "Museum of Science and Industry". The 1893 Columbian Exposition was a very special time for Chicago to show the spectacular White City that was built in record time. But, it also was a period that Chicago had some of its worst times, with a creepy serial killer on the loose, a disgruntled citizen who shot the Mayor of Chicago, and the Cold Storage Fire that took the lives of fifteen men! As a result of the great World's Fair, a fourth star was added to the Chicago Flag.

By the end of August 1894, Norm Doolan was probably one of the most popular firemen on the Chicago Fire Department. After working as the buggyman of the 14th battalion of the World's Fair, and getting so many firemen and their families in for free, everyone knew Norm. He was also known for working at the Cold Storage Building fire, and the funerals that followed. He already had the reputation of being on the first engine company to the Chicago Fire, or the "Big One" as Norm calls the Chicago Fire. They all knew him, including the Chief of the Brigade, Denis Swenie. He was known to be fast with a joke, and witty as hell. But, to get a reputation on this job you can't just be funny; he was a great pipeman who was very close to being killed on several occasions. But, if Norm Doolan will be remembered, it will be for what he did for the widows and orphans of the fallen firefighters who were killed in the Cold Storage fire. He went after Harlow Higinbotham the banker that tried to keep the fund money, like he was on a mission with fire in his eyes.

On the morning of September 1, 1894, a direct order came out transferring Chemical Engine 6, from Engine 19 to Truck Company 2 quarters located at 540 West Washington Street. A chemical engine is a two wheeled rig with a single tank that holds eighty gallons of bicarbonate of soda water. To put this chemical engine to work at a fire an acid is mixed with the soda, and pressure is quickly built up in the tank. This pressure then pushes the water through a small diameter hose line, and it is used on smaller fires with a good firefighter on the nozzle of a chemical engine who can put out a lot of fire, or hold it back until a positive water source is found. The Chemical Engine was made right here in Chicago.

Truck 2 is not a very wide firehouse, it was constructed for one truck company, but now with the Chief's buggy and a Chemical engine everything is like jammed. Truck 2 is an eighty-five foot Hayes Aerial ladder, the back end of the truck has a steering wheel for going around corners and it's called a "tiller". The Rig is pulled by two white horses. Also there had to be room made in the stables for one more horse, and in the bunk room two more beds for the officer and one firefighter, who came with Chemical 6.

The Officer on Chemical 6 was Lieutenant Cooper, and the firefighter was a young twenty-two year old kid called, William Ball. I liked him right away. He was young and full of energy, kind of reminded me of myself some thirty years ago. After all the house work was completed, I took this new firefighter into the back stables. Dutch was not very happy about sharing his stall, but that is the side of the fire house where the new Rig, the chemical engine was going to be located. I stopped and said hey to the new kid, "what do they call you, Ball, Billy, William, or what?" Oh, Mr. Doolan you can call me whatever you want, I am just happy to be working with you. "And you can call me Norm, son" I said.

So, I said to him, "Where do you come from Billy Ball? "Engine 19 on the southeast side," the kid said. I walked over to his side of the stable where he was admiring Truck 2's white horses. With a low voice I let him know that somehow, some way, someone got you on this Chemical engine, because this rig is not manned. Usually, when they put a chemical engine into a truck house the rig does not come with manpower; what happens is the Captain puts two of his firefighters on the rig. So, I said to the kid again, some one vouched for you to get to this fire house. Billy just looked back at me like he was confused, he didn't know what I was talking about, and went on his way.

I knew that he knew someone on the job, or in city hall, because I do know how things work on this job after thirty years. The Lieutenant also came on the Chemical Engine that is not the way it works. This started to bother me. I asked Chief Murphy and he said he didn't know was glad they were there and would take the extra men anytime. I tried to get the kid to talk, but he held tight. All he would say was that he wanted more fire duty, and was glad to be here. "How did you know there was a lot of fire duty here at Truck 2," I asked the kid?. "Oh, my uncle told me that this is one of the busiest fire houses in the city." I thought to myself, who's his uncle?

Everyone knows that firemen keep their engines and trucks in tip top condition. They polish the wheels, shine all the brass, oil the wheels and moving parts, clean the stalls, roll the hose, and exercise the horses, but what they wait for is the "BELL" . When the "GONG" sounds, firefighters, no matter where they are in and around the fire house they think about one thing "The Fire". While the bell rings out the numbers, someone get the address, the horses are hitched and we are out the door.

As the year of 1894 came to a close, the Chicago Fire Department through its many years of service, reported an unbelievable record-breaking number of fire calls. The annual report ending December 31, 1894 had data showing that fire alarms had risen to 1,229, for only one month. I call most of these fires nothing calls; garbage, or small fires by people burning in rubbish cans on the streets, and if the fire gets a little out of control they would pull a street fire box.

The increase in alarms was to be expected, because of the 1889 annexation of Chicago. The city's boundaries spread north to Devon Avenue where the city of Lakeview was located, then the city spread northwest taking in the Town of Jefferson, the towns of Cicero Lake, directly west of the city. To the south the city annexed the Village of Hyde Park down the shores of Lake Michigan all the way to 138th street. All this newly acquired land is now under the Chicago Fire Departments control and the watchful eyes of the Chief of the Brigade Denis Swenie.

Of the many truck companies in Chicago, Truck 2 was the busiest, and the main reason was that it followed five engine companies. The area just west of Truck 2 was made up of many haphazard buildings, with rooms for rent by the day. Fires in this area were occurring more and more, so the Chief of the brigade, Swenie, and Chief Campion decided to move Chemical Engine 6 from Engine 19, to Truck 2;s quarters. The Chief made sure that Chemical 6 had manpower, so Chief Campion sent two men with the Rig.

Suddenly the gong sounds, the Box alarm rigs out the numbers, and the Captain yells out, "That's just west of us on Washington Street." The horses begin to move to their places, the kid takes his horse and brings him around in front and hitches him up. The Lieutenant is up in his seat as they pull the Chemical Rig out the front doors. I finished hitching up Dutch and the Chief says, "Hey, I thought we were in front?" The buggy followed Chemical 6 west on Washington Street about three blocks. Smoke was rolling over the roof of a two- story brick apartment building. As the Chief and I approached we could see fire on the rear porches.

Chemical 6 is right in front of the building, and I can see the kid, Billy Ball leading out the rubber hose line from the engine. He disappeared into a gangway between the buildings. I pulled the buggy out of the way, because engine 5 would need to lead out. Chief Murphy said to get a line around the rear to back up Chemical 6. As I made it down the gang way the smoke began to change color, I thought the kid was hitting the fire, but when I got up on the rear porches the fire was out, and all that was left were some hot spots. Engine 5 took their line up to the rear porches and extinguished the remaining fire.

Lieutenant Cooper, and the kid began picking up their rubber hose line. Chief Murphy approached them and said, "Good job guys, you made a hell of a good stop." It doesn't matter who you are on the fire department everyone likes to hear that they did a good job, especially when it comes from the Chief Officer. I thought to myself, good job, "punk". We began picking up Engine 5's hose line, and retuned to our quarters. Back in Truck 2's fire house I looked around for the kid, but he wasn't on the apparatus floor. So I walked into the stables in the back, and there he was, watering the horses. I approached him, and said, "Hey, punk, you did a hell of good job back there on those porches." Very humbly he said, "Thanks Norm I had just enough water in the tank."

I asked the kid what type of horse was he watering. "Oh, his name is Spike, Norm, and he is a Latvian. He weighs 1200 pounds, and is 15hh; he continued saying he is a very good horse. He is very relaxed and takes good commands in the street." I was very impressed with how much the kid knew about the horse and about horses in general. He was also taught to take care of the horses so they would work for you. I began calling him, punk, he wasn't too sure about his new nick name, but took it in stride.

As the years went by the Chicago Fire Department grew with the annexation of all the new towns and all those fire companies that belonged to those towns were now Chicago fire companies. Chief Swenie made it a point to know each and every man on the department, and he kept a manuscript of each firefighter under his command. He was a very firm disciplinarian and was admired by his men. The Chief was a strong advocate of the merit system, long before it was popular with the city council.

There were eighty-five engine companies, twenty-five truck companies, four fire boats, and fifteen battalions. When money was available to the fire department, Chief Swenie tried to make living conditions in the fire houses better for the firefighters, because some of the fire houses still had dirt floors. Chief Swenie teamed up with the best, and the best was the Superintendent of the city's telegraph system, John Barrett. Telegraph poles were always getting knocked down in the city and Barrett convinced Swenie that all the wiring for the fire departments could be put underground. Many electricians said it could not be done, but with Chief Swenie was behind the plans to accomplish it and the plan went ahead with force. Well, it seemed to work well, and in a short time the many poles began to disappear from the downtown streets.

The dog days of summer in 1897 were some of the hottest that I can remember. Well, maybe it is just because I am now old, but it's not just me. Everyone was tired of the heat in the beginning of August. The temperature rose to the upper 90's every day.

The heat is very hard on the firefighters especially in a burning building. But, the heat is hard on all workers I think as I look out at the people who are working on the railroads and in construction jobs. These workers have to stay out in this heat all day long. I thought to myself, they all look forward to the end of the day too so they can make their way back to their homes.

This is the time of day that the night shift worker begins at the Northwestern Grain Elevator Company, located at Grand Avenue and the North Branch of the Chicago River. One of the employees, Edward Anderson, ran into the engine room and declared breathlessly, that he smelled smoke in the Elevator. Engineer Walter Grubb had just started his night shift and heard Anderson say that he smelled smoke. He flew out of the chair and wasted no time talking. As he past the clock in the engine room he noticed that it was just before 5:30 pm. George Avery was on the steps when Grubb said to him in a firm voice, "Summon the fire department right now!". Grubb looked up and said, "I don't think there is no fire in the grain bins." But they were below the bin floors and as he continued to move up, the atmosphere quickly began to get keen when he reached the landing on the bin floor. Grubb stepped in where he could better survey the bin floors. He saw curls of flames and smoke bursting through the floors and walls. "Oh, my God!" he yelled.

One look was enough; he ran down the stairs three steps at a time. He ran into the night watchman and yelled "Run for your lives, the bin floors are were about to go!". The watchman knew what Grubb meant and did not need a second warning. They ran down stairs to the main floor, fled into the engine room and out the door to the outside. They were both struggling for air as they both looked up. The cupola and the upper part of the building was a mass of flames.

In the fire house, a box alarm began ringing. The Captain yelled out, "That's our box, boys. Let's hitch them up." I had Dutch ready in less than a minute, and we were out the door headed west to Halsted, and once we turned north on Halsted Street we could see heavy smoke. I yelled, "Ya, ya," to Dutch as he began to strain against his collar faster and faster.

When we reached Grand Avenue you could now see flames on the top of the Grain Elevator. Chief Murphy said, "Go straight to the Box, Norm over the viaduct on the left side of the street". Chief Murphy saw the volume of fire, and he knew the dangers of a grain elevator. Chief Murphy almost jumped out of the buggy before I stopped at the street Box, he immediately opened the Box and sounded a 4-11 alarm.

As I turned the buggy around we could see all the engines and trucks begin to cross over the maze of railroad tracks. You could hear the clanging of their gongs. There was now panic in the air outside the elevator. It had greatly changed, and men by the railroad cars were yelling and screaming, "Get out of the area now, it's going to blow.!" The Northwestern Grain Elevator faces the North Branch of the Chicago River, and for blocks on the west side there are hundreds of loaded and empty freight and passenger railroad cars. These cars ran alongside the freight houses, and the spread of fire would mean sure destruction of all these buildings.

Chief Swenie arrived at the scene; the elevator was now burning fiercely at the top and the roof seamed like it was almost gone. The Chief reasoned with his officers on the scene that if there was to be an explosion the force would find a vent through the weakest part, in this case, the roof, because the roof was almost gone.

The orders went out to the men; "No one should be within sixty feet of the elevator. Spread the word." The Chief told his officers. I made my way around the people watching from Grand Avenue. Hundreds of people were leaving work and were now watching the fire. About thirty feet from the elevators north end was a branch of the Jung Brewing Company, a long low one-story building used for freight purposes. When Engine Company 27 arrived at the scene, Captain Bowmen could see the flames issuing from the top of the building. He gave an order to lead out a 2 ½ inch hose line on to the roof of the brewery and take the hydrant on Grand Avenue. Engine 27 had their water right away. Engine Company 3 arrived at about the same time as Engine 27, but came in from the west on Grand Avenue. Lieutenant Noon gave his order to lead out along the west side of the brewery.

I began yelling from the top to the firefighters that the orders were to stay at least sixty feet away from the grain elevator. As other engines began to arrive they too began following Engine 3 down the embankment with their lead outs and along the west side of the brewery. As Firefighter John Coogan of Engine Company 3, was leading out down the embankment he saw his wife on the Grand Avenue viaduct. She yelled to him, and he gave a wave back, and threw her a kiss. Also firefighter Straman saw his wife and sister up on the viaduct. They yelled to him to be careful and he replied, "All right, Honey." They dragged their hose line up as close as they could to the burning elevator. Lieutenant Noon gave the order to send the water on engine 3's, 2 ½ inch line. Soon the hose line began to fill, and the air gushed out the nozzle, followed by the water. Now we had two fire streams on the burning structure, working the North and west sides of the elevator.

We can hear and see the fireboat, Engine 37 (The Yosemite) begin to pull in, but there is a tug-boat, the D.P. Hall, moored right in front of the burning elevator. Captain Buckley of Engine 37 yelled, " I can't get close enough." And, from out of nowhere came Commander James Berry. He jumped in the tug, started the engines and moved the D. P. Hall out of the way. The (Yosemite) began throwing a 4 ½ inch stream of water on the fire from one of its deck guns. Now there are five hand lines on the fire plus the

84

fire boat. There are eleven engines on the bank of the River. I jumped down and grabbed hold of Engine 5's hose line, because they only had two guys pulling on their line. Firefighter Billy Hanley turned around and said, "Hey Norm, thanks for the help."

As we stretched the line closer to the burning elevator I looked up, and behind the flames you could see the outline of the roof. I don't like the looks of this one, I said to myself as we moved the line closer. Then sections of the roof and walls began to fall, crashing down sending showers of flaming embers into the air. Then the Lieutenant yelled to send the water on Engine 5's line, I turned back to repeat the order to send the water, on Engine 5's line. Suddenly there was a great light, followed by a loud boom, I turned toward Billy Hanley, but I couldn't see him. Then I heard someone yell, "Run for your lives!!!". I was knocked down by an explosion or by the actual falling walls. I am not sure which swept me off my feet.

I crawled along blindly in the smoke and dust. All you could hear was several men groaning and calling for help. All the time we were being showered by burning dust and embers. I continued crawling and soon I could see the viaduct. My left leg was badly injured and my face and hands were burned. Two firefighters picked me up, and took me under the viaduct next to the river. I now knew that many firefighters were killed or severely injured by the explosion. Thousands of people watched the horror unfold before their eyes, and many spectators were also injured by the explosion. Glass in homes and factories were broken in over a one mile area in ether direction. All the hospitals were full, so I was taken to my home on west 51st Street. When Nancy saw me she just cried. I told her I was okay, but there are many who are not.

The fire burned for several hours. I was later informed that Chiefs, Musham, Campion, and even the Chief of the Brigade Denis Swenie were all injured by the explosion.

As the night went on they continued to pour water on what remained of the sixty-seven foot structure. The injured was at a count of 27 firefighters and 12 civilians. There were two dead firefighters and one was missing, of the twenty- seven injured firefighters six of them were in critical condition and were not supposed to live until the morning. The missing firefighter is Chief Swenie's buggy man, Thomas Monaghan. Witnesses say that it is possible that at the time of the explosion, he could have been blown into the River or covered by the debris. He was Chief Swenie's driver for seventeen years. He joined the department in 1880 and was assigned to Swenie which is the only duty he ever performed on the fire department. Captain Buckley of the fire boat, Yosemite, dragged the river bottom for hours looking for him. He was never found.

The bodies of Firefighters Jacob Straman, Jacob Schnur, and John Coogan, all of Engine Company 3, were taken to the morgue. At 4:10 pm on Friday August 6, 1897 Firefighter Charles Conway, of Engine Company 27, died from his injuries at the county hospital. In all six firefighters died in the line of duty; they made the ultimate sacrifice.

Tired, hungry, and sleepy Firefighters stood about the ruins, mourning the deaths of their comrades while others directed their engine streams of water at the smoking black piles of timber. With their axes in hand they dug through the piles of debris expecting to finding the bodies of firefighters who were thought to have been caught under the falling walls. Chief Swenie appeared at his office, very sore from his many bruises, and walking with a bad limp. A portion of his shoe had to be cut away to relieve the pressure on the burned portion of his foot. His face was red and blistered. Chief Swenie was very sad about the loss of his driver, Firefighter Thomas Monaghan.

Chief Swenie was criticized for allowing the firefighters to get in so close to the burning Grain Elevator. The Chief was interviewed about this allegation and he replied by saying there were no firefighters within sixty feet of the elevator when the walls fell. "I was there myself," he said, "and if I had thought there was any danger, do you think I would have permitted my men or myself to be within reach of that danger? . The Chief continued the interview, "Firefighting is a very hazardous occupation at its best, and when men join the department they have thought this all over. They are told of the dangers. Their efforts are always accompanied by more or less danger. The wisest general that has lived cannot always accomplish results without some loss. On August 19, 1897, the last firefighter injured in the Grain Elevator fire, Firefighter William Hanley, died from his injuries incurred at the Grain Elevator fire.

Norm announced, "I will remain at home in the care of wife, Nancy. I will no longer go back to firefighting, because this one was too close of a call. After just over thirty years it is the time for my retirement. I had a long great career on the Chicago Fire Department."

Norm Doolan will always be best remembered for his great honor. But also his bravery and dedication to the job he loved.

The Retirement Party

The young fireman, Billy Ball, who became best friends with Norm Doolan, still could not get over the fact that he was not going to return to the fire department. For over a month, the punk, visited Norm at his home. Every time he left Norm's house, all he thought of was that working with him was probably the greatest experience of his life. Although it was hard to grasp that he would not return to the job, the punk did understand Norm's reasons for retiring. Norm Doolan was critically injured in 1877 at the Marshall Fields Fire were he lost his best friend, and two other firemen. Now, after being burned on his face, hands, and legs, having broken his arm and experiencing a hearing loss in one ear, Norm Doolan had a good reason to stay at home with his wife and three children.

Fireman Ball wanted to do something for Norm. He went to see his Uncle, Chief John Campion, and asked him is there a way that we could throw a party for Doolan. Chief Campion said, "I will ask Chiefs Swenie and Musham, but in the meantime, you get back to Doolan and see if he wants a party. Billy ball went to see Norm and Norm said, "I am flattered by the notion that a party would be thrown for me. But, I will agree to the party only if all the proceeds go to the widows and children of the six firemen who lost their lives and for those who were injured at the Northwestern Elevator Explosion.

The word went out, and spread faster than the fire that raced through Chicago in 1871. Everyone wanted to go to this party. Fireman Ball went to Norm's favorite place, The Midway Lounge and Banquet Hall to ask if the party could be held at this Hall.. He told the owner that the party was for Norm Doolan, and any of the proceeds from the party would go to the widows and children of the six firemen that were killed at the elevator explosion. The owner of the restaurant said not only can you have the party here, but there is no charge for the hall.

The date for the party was set for September 16, 1897 and because it was to be a fund raiser, a meat company located in the Stockyards donated the mat, a hotel donated freshly baked rolls and bread and the beer was donated by The Koller Brewing Company from the stockyards, located at 39th and Racine. Tickets for the affair were 50 cents each.

Saturday September 16, 1897 arrived and .it was a perfect evening. The hall was decorated, filled with tables that were covered with white linen table cloths. On the west end of the hall was the head table positioned on a raised platform of about one foot so those who sat in the back of the room were able to see Norm.. Alongside the head table was an area where three-piece Irish band set up. The band had a fiddler and of course the bagpipers.

At 6:00 pm the people began arriving and filing into the hall. Norm and Nancy met everyone at the entrance door. All the fire department chief officers were there, and any fireman that was lucky enough to get some time off duty. Cocktail hour was from 6:00 to 7:00pm. Fireman Ball made the introductions for the Chief Officers who sat at the head table, followed by the widows and some of the children of the elevator fire.

There was silence for a minute, and then the bagpipers began to play in the back of the hall. They then began marching up to the head table with Norm Doolan and his wife Nancy joining them. Everyone in the hall were standing up and clapping. Food was served, and a prayer was said by the fire department Chaplin Father John McNalis. The food was served family style with trays of fried chicken, beef, sausage, and plenty of foaming pitchers of Topaz Beer.

After dinner there were a speech given about Norm from the Chief of the Brigade, Denis Swenie. Norm also spoke thanking everyone for coming, especially Fireman Bill Ball. As the night went on, the music played and most firemen made their way up to the bar to tell fire stories to one another. But, some firemen wandered around looking for old friends to talk to. It was a grand time, and fun was had by all.

As a result of the party, there was close to one thousand dollars that was collected for the widows and children and the injured firemen. I was able to distribute the money to all those who it had been given for. It was not enough, but I am sure it will help them in their time of need. Even though I was officially retired and off the Chicago Fire Department, I had to go back and see the boys.

As the years went by times were getting tough again, and the morale of the job was falling to an all time low. The job was changing; it was hard to get any time off other than the three hours allotted for meals. There haven't been many recruits joining the department, mainly because of the one platoon system.

Firemen want time off to spend with there families, but were only allowed three hours per day. If you were an "in guy" and the Captain liked you, then he would give you the night off every once in a while. Some guys would get a full day off, like Christmas, because they were the favorites of the Battalion Chief. To many of the firemen Christmas day was not that important, because it had only been a federal holiday since 1870. But, firemen with children were allowed some extra time off, maybe to have their meal and open some presents. Otherwise, Christmas Day was just another cold winter day in Chicago.

During the turn of the century, men, women, and often times their children worked long hours in some of the most unsafe work conditions. Most people struggled to pay their rent and put food on the table. It just seemed that with very small wages a working person just couldn't get ahead, and there wasn't much to look forward to other than getting older and dying. The average age of a man was forty-seven years old. Workers in the spring of 1900 began joining together in Chicago, and all over America, a nationwide union movement to counter the terrible working conditions across this country. I was one of the lucky ones. My children are older and I am retired, and I have a small business in my barn repairing wagons.

My friend, Lieutenant Henry Bassett, knew if he called me to give him a helping hand that I would. He has asked if I would help band the firemen of Chicago together for their mutual benefit. We scheduled a meeting at my home at 51st street and Pulina Avenue, just south of the Chicago Stockyards. Henry came down during his meal brake; Nancy made some sandwiches and coffee. Henry said, "I came to you because you know people on this job and they respect you, and you can help me organize the firemen," Henry said,. "It's about time that firemen band together"

A fireman's salary was not that bad, but of course it was lower than that of skilled labor. The main reason that the morale is so low is because all firemen labor under the "continuous duty system" which requires firemen and officers to live in the firehouse. The only time a fireman can leave would be for meals three times a day.

If a fireman did his job well, and the captain liked him, maybe he would stretch his meal time a little. If the Captain and Battalion Chief liked you, you might get a routine day off, maybe twice a month. If the fireman or officer was really liked by the Chief, then maybe he would get a short vacation break. "That kind of working condition stinks," Henry said.

If the Fire Department was to let half of Department work one day and the other half work the next day it would be so much better for the firemen and the city. I said, "That's a great idea, but the city would have to hire more men." "Yes, but in the long run, it will be a better force. The department really wouldn't have to hire that many more firemen. There is 1,142 firemen on the job now, so 570 could work one day and 570 the next day. It can be done, Norm," Henry said. "This can be done with two platoons". We shook hands and I said, "I will talk to some people because, I like the idea."

I did know a lot of people on the Chicago Fire Department but I also knew that the upper echelon of the Fire Department was not going to like the idea of organizing the firemen into a union. I did agree with Henry Bassett that you just can't keep working a person like a field horse. S sooner or later he is going to get mad, and he then will revolt.

The first person I talked to was Chief Murphy, who I could ask just about anything. I asked him about organizing of the firemen and he replied, "Norm, we don't like change on this job. This two platoon system would cost money and that is when your big trouble will come." I knew that Chief Murphy was right about one thing, firemen don't like change.

After talking to Chief Murphy I was able to talk to the Chief of the Brigade, Dennis Swenie. As soon as I mentioned Lieutenant Henry Bassett's name, the Chief said he thought this guy was a trouble maker. "He has been trying to change the job ever since he got on the job" Swenie said. In a very loud voice he informed me that "no way is there going to be any organization, other than the Chicago Fire Department," the Chief said!

That was strike two. I know my old Captain, who is now the First Assistant Fire Marshal and Department Inspector would be able to help so I went to see him. At first he was glad to see me, until I mentioned Lt. Henry Bassett's name, and he went into a rage. Chief Musham began yelling at me saying, "You and that Bassett guy are trying to undermine the authority of the Chief's on this Department". He continued about allowing the fireman to go to a two platoon system was out of the question. "Now, get out of my office!" he yelled. That is when I drew the line. I said, "For your information Chief, I love this job. The Fire Department has been my whole life and it is not my intention to undermine the Fire Department. Just think about it; firemen have no life. They never go home. They can't even have a relationship or start a family. Who would marry a guy who never comes out of the firehouse? And one more thing, Chief, you are not my boss anymore. "

Well after three strikes you're out. I met with Henry again and he said, "All we can do is to talk to the firemen and see if they want to organize." So, I went to see the firemen on the South side and Henry went to the North and West sides. The first firehouse I visited was Engine Company 59. A good friend, Captain Collins, is in that firehouse and we go way back. I told him what I had done so far with Chief Swenie and Musham and what their reactions were. Captain Collins agreed that we should get together, but he was also afraid of what could happen. "We could get fired, Norm", Collins said.

As time went by we were able to talk to the firemen and their officers. They all agreed a two platoon system would be great and even greater to have a whole day off. The only way to get the city to agree was if we all banded together in one voice of solidarity! This new militant attitude grew from one firehouse to another, from fireman to fireman and, the firemen were mad!

This was too much for Fire Marshal Swenie and he resigned from the Department on June 1, 1901. He was a fireman for 52 years and saw tremendous changes in the Fire Department, many of them in his 22 year reign as a Fire Marshal. After Chief Swenie's resignation, William H. Musham was appointed Fire Marshal and John Campion were appointed First Assistant Fire Marshal and the Department Inspector. One thing was certain; the majority of the department joined the organization.

In September of 1901, Chicago Firemen formed The Independent Firemen's Association and they made Henry Basset the President. This young association had its problems with the new Chief Fire Marshal Musham. The Chief stood his ground about the two platoon system! Even though the firemen were now organized, and the firemen's association was a reality, things did not change. But, the most important part of the association, and what Lieutenant Henry Bassett wanted was that firemen were now together, with one voice. This two platoon system can work, and all the firemen want an end to this one continuous system. Most of the firemen that I knew liked Chief Musham, because he was one of them. The Chief was a "Blue Shirt" type of guy, who never forgot where he came from, and as an officer of undoubted efficiency. But, in no time at all, the rank and file quickly took a fierce disliking to Musham's heavy handed rules and regulations, because of his opposition to the two platoon system.

In 1900, we had a fireman's ball for the benefit of the pension fund, and it was so successful that we were planning a second annual ball at the Coliseum at 1501 South Wabash, just south of down town. I have been involved with this year's event, because it raised money for our injured firemen and those who made the supreme sacrifice. The second annual Fireman's Ball was to be on Wednesday October 30, 1901, it was a night of fun for all those who attended. It was a who's- who type of event, the Mayor, Aldermen and business men and women came in their finest. The firemen wore their uniforms. Chief Musham was there, but would not talk to me because of my involvement with The Fireman's Association and Henry Bassett. As a matter of fact, Chief Musham stayed on the other side of the Coliseum with the politicians and businessmen. Chief Musham totally opposed The Firemen's Association, because the businessmen of Chicago knew that this two platoon system would cost money, and they would keep the pressure on Chief Musham to staunchly oppose it.

The second annual ball was a total success, and helped raise funds for the widows and children who had lost their husbands and fathers, something that I believed was a good thing. Just in the last three-years nineteen firemen have been killed in the line of duty, leaving seventeen widows and thirty-eight children without a provider. The Beneficiary Act gave each widow thirty dollars per month, and each child received six dollars per month up to the age of sixteen years old. My wife Nancy and I would go to the churches and schools that were having rummage sales and we bought coats, clothes, shoes, hats and anything that was in so-so condition. Nancy would find out which widows or orphans who were the neediest, and we would give them what we bought at those garage sales.

I have always remained in contact with Henry Bassett to find out what was going on with the fire department. Between Henry and Chief Jim Horan of the 5th Battalion they kept me up to date. Chief Horan has been a good friend of mine. He has helped me out with many issues concerning the widows, and he has helped me in the past with that banker, Harlow Higinbotham, the low-life that tried to keep the funds from the widows and children of the Cold Storage fire in 1893. Chief Horan informed me that the firemen were frustrated with the job Chief Musham was doing. "Everything is a fight, and he is mad as hell at me," Horan said, "because I joined The Firemen's Association with many other officers on the job. Chief Horan knew that sooner than later the Chicago Fire Department was going to have a two platoon system, and he also knew it would be good for the job.

Musham had alienated most of his officers in the last two years and he thinks that they are all trying to deliberately make him look bad. He was actually doing it to himself. Chief Musham has built a wall between himself and his officers, the guys that he depended on to help him do his job.

The fire officers knew that the chief was making mistakes one after another. He was a hell of a fire chief, but could not keep up with the administrative part of the job. So, with that in mine, some of the officers and firemen made some calls to city officials and insurance executives, complaining about his performance as Chief Fire Marshal.

Word got back to Chief Musham that some of the officers went over his head telling outsiders about the job he was doing, and this was a no-no on the Chicago Fire Department. Chief Musham identified six of these firemen and officers, and all six of them were ordered to appear before a trial board in his office at city hall, on Wednesday December 30, 1903 at 14:00 hours.

Henry Bassett informed me about this trial that was going to be held at city hall. He also informed me that I knew at least two of the guys that were going to trial. I asked Henry why he wasn't involved in this court trouble because he was the President of The Fireman's Association. Henry said, "Because I did not make any of the calls that got the chief in an uproar. But, I will be at the trial as the representative of the men who were going to appear before the trial board. "Would you like to come with, Norm?" he asked.

"Absolutely," I replied. I was very interested in this "Kangaroo" court that Chief Musham was about, because I knew Musham was mad as hell and he was out to do "business" with these guys on the first floor office of city hall. I met Henry in the "Loop" on Wednesday December 30, 1903, and he told me that Chief Horan said that the guys that are going on trial will be lucky to keep their jobs. The "Loop" is the nickname for Chicago's downtown business district. The streets included in the "Loop" are roughly those in the circle of Chicago's elevated rail system called the "El"

The "Loop" was very busy that day, and I asked Henry, "What is going on?" He said. "You mean to tell me that you don't know that Eddie Foy was back in his home town Chicago, and performing in the musical comedy Mr. Blue Beard. There is a matinee performance at the brand new Iroquois Theater over at Randolph and Dearborn Streets today"

"Oh, yes I said, "Now I remember, because Nancy was going to take our girls, Debbie and Susan, to see that play some day this week. As we walked down LaSalle Street toward city hall, Henry continued to tell me that he has a friend who is working at the Iroquois Theater. He told me that this theater is absolutely fireproof and that they even have a billboard sign on Dearborn Street.

"Well," I said to Henry "Absolutely fireproof. I don't think there is anything that's totally fireproof. Always remember Henry that I was at the "Big One, the Chicago Fire. Henry just laughed at me and said, "You are such a skeptic, Norm. You know that he was talking about this," I said, "I remember talking to Patrick Jennings, he's the Captain of Engine Company 13, and he did a walk through of the Iroquois Theater with the firemen on his company in late November. He told me that there was no fire alarm system, sprinkler system, and no exit signs visible in the theater.

Henry said, "That was a month ago. They probably have all that fixed by now," as we walked through the Randolph Street doors of city hall for the trial.

Just a few blocks east of city hall on Randolph Street, hundreds of people, mainly women and children were lining up and began filing into the Iroquois Theater. Despite the sub freezing temperatures and the icy sidewalks everyone wanted to see Eddie Foy and the play *Mr. Bluebeard*. The entrance to the Iroquois Theater had five pairs of double mahogany doors that led into a marble walled vestibule, with eighteen foot ceilings. The special pride of this breath taking entrance was the richly appointed Grand Stair Hall which led up to the dress circle balconies.

Lucky ticket holders went straight through the foyer and into the orchestra section of seats, also called the parquet. Once the ticket holder reached the top floor by way of the Grand Stair Hall, they still had to navigate the stairway that turns to reach the second balcony of the auditorium. The orchestra section on the main floor of the theater had seats faced west and there were nineteen rows that held seven hundred and forty-four people. These were the best seats in the house. The rows were slightly curved, and were divided by three carpeted aisles.

The first balcony, or dress circle, had about four hundred and seventy-five seats, with the remaining seats in the second balcony which had some five hundred and five seats. The Building Department of Chicago cleared the theater for one thousand seven hundred and twenty-four patrons. The interior of the theater was just breath taking to most theatergoers; the size of the stage was massive, seventy feet deep and ninety feet wide. The paneling on the walls was French style, while the color scheme was American beauty red, with neutral tints of green and gold.

High above the theater was a large skylight of tinted glass which gave an illusion of sparkling stars. The skylight was also intended to vent the building of gaseous fumes, and flames in the case of a fire. The children were speechless with awe as their parents led them to their seats, for the first act was about to begin. Back stage there were nearly three hundred performers, plus two hundred members of the crew, like wardrobe people, scene movers, lighting operators, electricians, and carpenters.

The performance began, and the House Manager, George Dunsberry, made a final routine check. The box office enjoyed a larger crowd than expected, and there were over two hundred standees that paid to get in to see Eddie Foy. Many of the standees were in the upper balconies, and to keep them from sneaking down to the more expensive seats, accordion gates were closed and locked during the performances.

Altogether when the curtain went up there were about two thousand three hundred souls packed into the Iroquois Theater on that Wednesday December 30, 1903. The first act started and it was very entertaining and enjoyed by all. There was an intermission at the end of the first. Right away people stood up and began moving around, especially the people in the aisles. They began moving around, stretching their legs; many moved up and cleared the aisle. After a short intermission, the second act began. Just before 3:00pm, Eddie Foy came out and did his Sister Anne sketch with a pet elephant. The audience just loved the act. Then the stage curtain began to go up, and at this time it was customary to turn off the lights, all the lights. Only a soft bluish tint illuminated the theater. Back stage about fifteen feet above the stage was an iron bridge. On that bridge was a flood light with blue gel. It was a calcium arc light powered by electricity. There is an opening above the arc light in a hood about two inches in diameter. This light needs 110 volts to operate, and when lit, the light will generate about four thousand degrees of heat. The light is handled by an operator to direct the beam of light. During each performance the light is moved very slowly up, down, or sideways to illuminate the stage.

The light was aimed across the stage, and this was the cue for the dancers to begin dancing to, *In the Pale Moonlight*. For some unaccountable reason the operator moved away from the arc light for one moment. Suddenly there was a flash of sparks in the back of the arc light where the wires were connected. The flash of sparks was seen by two actors across the stage, and just then a curtain next to the light caught fire. An electrician noticed the blaze traveling up the edge of the curtain, and he yelled at another electrician on the other side of the stage, "Hurry, put it out! The man ran up the ladder, and reached out trying to clap the burning curtain with his hands. Just then another stage hand spotted the burning curtain, and he also yelled, "Put it out! "I am trying," he answered, as he continued slapping the curtain, and burning his hands.

The flames shot a foot or so upward and extended to other curtains high above him. A chemical fire extinguisher was handed up to the electrician on the ladder. He tried using the tube fire extinguisher, but it only blew back down on him. The theater had house firemen Bill Sallars; he also tried one of the chemical fire extinguishers but it too failed. Sallars yelled down to lower the asbestos curtain, because now the fire had head way. The musicians continued to play and the actors attempted to dance across the stage, as glowing embers fell from the burning curtains high above.

Eddie Foy, after hearing the commotion, came out on stage to calm the audience; praying that the fire could be extinguished. There was some confusion on how to lower the asbestos curtain and, as it began dropping down the left side of the curtain caught on a spot light and the curtain went down on an angle and stopped. The stage hands and actors began running for their lives toward the stage door that leads into the alley behind the theater. Opening the stage door caused an on-rush of air; that draft of air drew the fire outward and out into the audience.

Because of the second act called for darkness, there were no lights in the theater. Heavy draperies covered the exit signs, because it would distract from the stage. There was no telephone backstage, and no fire alarm. One stage hand ran down Dearborn Street to Engine Company 13's fire house which was a block away. On stage, Eddie Foy fell to the floor when large flaming fragments fell down on him. A large billow of flame leaped over Foy and out into the large auditorium. Then women screamed as loud as they could, and every one rose to their feet. The aisles were filled with people sitting on the floor and the steps. Suddenly, hundreds of people began rushing for the doors. All you could hear were the screams as a mass of people stampeding over one another.

The stagehand arrived at Engine 13, and began tapping on the glass window, yelling, "Fire, fire at the Iroquois Theater." Firemen Michael Corrigan opened the door and sounded the alarm. Within seconds the horses were hitched and the engine was out the door. An alarm in the business district automatically drew five horse drawn engine companies, two truck companies, and two chemical engines within minutes.

Meanwhile Chief Musham's disciplinary hearing was going on; we were not allowed in the room because Doolan said Musham and Bassett were trouble makers. The Chief Fire Marshal continued to blow off steam about the six men that were on trial. Suddenly the fire alarm register in Chief Musham's office began to sound out a box alarm. The hearing stopped for a few seconds and all the officers and firemen began counting the number of bells. Then Chief Musham jumped to his feet, and said in a very loud voice, "That box is at State and Randolph." They all pushed away from the table at once "Let's go," Musham yelled.

As they all came rushing out the Chief's door, someone yelled to us, "There is a box alarm at State and Randolph." Henry and I jumped to our feet. I looked to Henry and said, "Once firemen, always a firemen," and we followed Chief Musham and the firemen out onto the Randolph Street side of City Hall.

It's a funny thing about firemen, and it's almost hard to believe, all the animosities and anger is all gone when the bell rings and it comes time to battle a fire. When Engine Company 13 arrived on the scene of the Iroquois Theater, they saw no fire or smoke and there were only a few people out in front of the theater. As the firemen began walking through the front Mahogany doors, someone said, "I bet this is a false alarm." Then almost instantly the firemen's noses told them of the horror that they knew they were about to find behind the closed and locked doors of the Iroquois Theater.

We arrived minutes behind Engine 13. Chief Musham followed the firemen into the lobby of the theater. Chief Musham saw the bodies of three children lying on the floor, "Oh, dear Jesus," he yelled in a loud voice. The Chief ordered his driver to request a 3-11 alarm and call for every ambulance in the city to respond to the Iroquois Theater.

The firemen's orders were to get the doors open that lead into the theater. Because of the way the doors opened inward, firemen had to pry and chop with their axes in an effort to get into where they could hear the muffled cries of women and children. The first set of doors were pulled open, and heat and black smoke poured out into the lobby. The smoke caused the firemen to retreat, because of the stench of the burning bodies and just the overall sight. After the smoke thinned out a bit it revealed the piles of children, men, and women jammed together and stacked four feet deep. It was a mass of crisp human beings with headless trunks, legs and arms missing. The smell of burned human flesh filled the air and such a sight could never be forgotten in a life time.

Firemen began the gruesome task of removing the bodies off the top of the pile in the doorway, in order to get their fire hoses into the theater to extinguish the fire still burning on the stage. The bodies were moved on to the foyer floor, and then they were removed to the ambulances and hose wagons lined up on Randolph Street. A priest in the lobby was begging people at the top of his voice, to put their trust in God, and to try to calm them.

Chief Horan came out in front; I spied him at once, because the look on his face told the story of what was inside. The Chief approached me, "Norm "he said, " we need blankets, sheets, anything to cover them up with."

There were two men standing next to me, I said, "Will you help me?" "Absolutely," they replied. The three of us ran to the Marshall Fields store a block away on State Street. We grabbed as many blankets as we could carry, and returned to the scene.

Big, strong, masculine men were standing in the street with tears falling from their eyes, as they called out the names of their loved ones. We began loading the dead onto wagons, putting on as many as the wagon will hold. As the wagon pulled away, another one was brought into position and as the night wore on darkness made it harder to work. A nearby hardware store owner supplied many lanterns to be used in the dark theater.

The firemen made their way up the marble stairs to the upper balconies, where they found bodies in the stairway where the two balconies came together. There were about one hundred fifty, or maybe two hundred bodies stacked like cord wood ten high. The people inside the balcony were still sitting in their seats with their heads leaning forward against the seat in front of them; they were terribly burned. The victims in the balconies were burned by the ball of fire that extended under the asbestos curtain. On the other side of the balconies were the exits without lights. Heavy draperies covered the exits to the fire escape. After the smoke filled up the theater, the hot gases began chocking the children. Mothers screamed as the crushing stampede tried desperately to get to the exit doors on the fire escape. But, the fire escapes were not finished; people panicking pushed their way out onto the fire escape, only to be pushed off the third floor platform to their deaths in the alley below.

Just across the alley at the Northwestern University Law School building, some law students heard the commotion in the alley, they couldn't believe their eyes. Some painters were working in the hallway so the law students and painters took planks and stretched them across the alley to the fire escape platform of the theater. Many people made it across, and some fell from the planks. Many people were able to make it across before a ball of fire blew out the exit doors into the alley. A total of one hundred twenty three bodies were recovered from the alley behind the Iroquois Theater. The newspapers called it Death Alley.

The firemen pushed forward into the auditorium with their hose lines, and the fire was extinguished and the smoke began to clear away. For the first time the firemen had a good look at what was burning, fabric curtains and wooden seats filled with Hemp. But the fire load that produced the most smoke was the human bodies. As the cold night continued on, the bodies were now being removed swiftly. There were many Chicago fire ambulances and hose carts that went into action.

Interior view of the Iroquois showing the stage area where fire ignited draperies and spread quickly to combustible scenery props.

The dead were moved in a matter of hours to the morgue and to local hospitals. Henry Bassett and I helped load bodies onto the wagons. You were always hoping someone would say this is the last one; but they just kept coming. The work was done in almost silence. Even after what had occurred, the bodies had to be removed. That's what we do; we are firemen and this one will remain in our hearts and minds forever. When the toll was made of how many victims, it was unbelievable. Six hundred and two people were dead, and over two hundred and fifty were injured. But, the most heartbreaking news was that of the dead, two hundred and twelve of them were children.

The news flashed across the nation quickly which made a very grim ending to 1903. This was one New Year's Eve in Chicago where there would be no bells ringing in the new year or numerous celebrations. Mayor Carter Harrison II proclaimed New Year's Eve as a time of mourning.

On January 2, 1904 Chicago observed an official day of mourning. People started talking about some of the slimy facts that now were coming to light from the Iroquois Theater. Chicago's shock and disbelief turned into rage. A coroner's jury ordered Mayor Harrison, Chief Mushm and City theater officials held for grand jury action.

A few days after the Iroquois theater fire, I went to see Al Lannon, the Captain of Engine Company 50. This fire house was close to my home. While we were having coffee, I was told that Chief Musham had the responsibility to inspect the interior of the new Iroquois Theater personally, and he did not. Captain Lannon told me that there will be no tears shed from the firemen, and they don't care if Chief Musham was to be fired. The citizens of Chicago want someone to be accountable for all of those people who died so horribly and inexcusably in the Iroquois Theater fire.

The public knew exactly who to point their fingers at for the slaughter of innocents. From the churches throughout the area, Reverends proclaimed, "Let no guilty man escape". Well guess what, the rage settled down in the next few months and they all got themselves a very good attorney. When the trial was over, nobody went to jail, and there were no penalties or fines. The only thing that they couldn't clear up was their conscious. They would have to live with for the rest of their lives.

Chief Musham was replaced shortly after the trial on the eighth day of October 1904 which was the twenty- ninth anniversary of the Chicago Fire. I felt bad about Chief Musham's premature resignation, on the same day of the Chicago Fire. He had gallantly fought that fire as the Captain of Engine 6, the "little Giant", with me. Chief Musham also had great ideas for a high pressure water system. The system could connect the fire boats to the water mains in Chicago's business district and convey water by direct pressure to the area of the fire where the engines could then send the water to the firemen.

There were a few firemen that met Chief Musham at Engine 6; to bid him farewell in his retirement. They had a cake and coffee type of thing, nothing big. I stopped to shake the hand of my old Captain, and William Musham, the now retired Chief, gave me a wink and nod in our old firehouse. He was my Captain and h e taught me how to be a good fireman; I won't forget him.

On Monday, October 17, 1904, John Campion was appointed the Chief Fire Marshal of the Chicago Fire Department. He is a veteran of the Great Chicago Fire. It has been said that he is one fearless fireman as he has made over 350 rescues. I called Henry Bassett, President of the Firemen's Association, and he was very excited about Chief Campion's appointment. He said that Chief Campion came up through the ranks and we can work with this guy.

All Henry was thinking about was the two platoon system. "Chief Campion knows what the conditions are like in the firehouses, twelve and fourteen firemen living in a one room dorm with one washroom, and that needs to be fixed." I said, He also told me that as an example of the living conditions in the firehouse, Chief Campion's son Frank, the Captain of Engine Company 7, has been in and out of the County Hospital suffering from delirium. "But, Norm," Henry said, "I have a friend who is a nurse at County Hospital and she informed me that Frank Campion is being treated as an alcoholic, not for delirium." I know Chief Campion will work with us for the two platoon system," Henry said with a little snicker in his voice. I said, "Henry, you wouldn't use what the nurse told you about his son's hospitalizations on him, would you?"

Even though I am not on the job anymore, and I don't go to fires, I still get excited when something new occurs on the Fire Department. I think I am lucky to still be able to see all the new changes, and still be a small part of the Chicago Fire Department. By the end of the year of 1904, the Chicago Fire Department was comprised of 17 battalions, and the uniform force was 1,326. There were 25 Fire Alarm Telegraph Operators, with a compliment of 512 horses. Henry Bassett was beginning to get some flack from the firemen about this two platoon business. "Are we going to get this or is it all bullshit about this Firemen's Association?" the firemen asked him.

President Henry Bassett made an appointment with the Chief of the Brigade, John Campion, to talk about the two platoon system. Chief Campion went on and on about how he might look into the platoon system, but not right away because he had too many other things to take care of. Henry couldn't go back to the members of the Firemen's Association and tell them the Chief might look into the two platoon system.

Henry leaned across his desk and suggested that they look right at the possibility of a two platoon system right now, before someone let's the newspapers know about where your son Frank is right now.

Chief Campion said to Henry, "you know that I was always for the two platoon system, and I think it will be one of my top priorities." With that, Henry Bassett bid the Chief farewell, shook hands and walked out of his office. I met up with Henry for lunch in the "loop" and after hearing the story, I almost fell off my chair laughing. Since when was Chief Campion so in favor of the two platoon system?

After several meetings with the Mayor, Chief Campion persuaded him that a two platoon system would be a good thing for the Fire Department. and also good for the citizens of Chicago, Mayor Dunne ordered Chief Campion to initiate the two platoon system on a trial basis only.

One week later, Chief Campion called Henry Bassett for a meeting in his City Hall office. The Chief informed Henry that the City was willing to give the two platoon system a try, but there will be no raises for anyone on the Department

The system will begin with a test in the First Battalion. If it does not work, they will go back to the one continuous platoon. The Chief continued to tell Henry that Engine Companies 1, 13, 10, 32 and 40 and Truck Companies 6 and 9 have been the selected companies for the test. They will work twelve hours on duty and they will be off duty for twelve hours.

I waited outside of City Hall on Randolph Street for Henry to come out of his meeting with the Chief Fire Marshal. I immediately saw a slight grin on Henry's face as he approached me and yelled out loud "Twelve on and twelve off", we hugged each other. "We have to get the word out now, Norm," he said. "I will go north and you go south."

I first stopped at my old stomping ground, Engine Company 6, "The Little Giant". I told the officers and firemen the news about twelve on and twelve off system. They couldn't believe it when I told them, and I asked them to get the news out on the wire. As fast as my horse could pull the wagon, I then went to Engine 59's firehouse at 818 West Exchange in the Stockyards and told my friend, Captain Collins and the firemen. Just think, twelve hours off to do anything you want to, sleep without being disturbed by bells ringing all day and night, it was almost too good to believe.

The test of the two platoon system began on August 4, 1906 in the 1st Battalion, but it wouldn't be long until all the firemen in Chicago would be on the two platoon system. In no time at all, the high morale that I once knew was back on the Chicago Fire Department. Lieutenant Henry Bassett is now the most popular guy on the job.

Lt. Henry Bassett was assigned to Engine 96 way out on the west side of Chicago, but because of his high exposure to this new platoon system, he was detailed to Engine Company 40 in the 1st Battalion. Chief Campion wanted him to be included in this new two platoon system. Engine Company 40 is located at 117 North Franklin Street just a little north of Washington Street. I liked Engine 40; it is a two bay firehouse with Truck Company 6 in the second bay, and it was easy for me to visit Henry

The two platoon system was working very well and all the firemen were happy about being off for twelve hours. This was especially true in the cold of Chicago winters. Engine Company 40 and Truck 6 are in the downtown Chicago business district although technically not in the "Loop". That area is called the "Iron Ring" because it is inside of the "El" tracks that travel Wells Street, Van Buren, Wabash and Lake Street in a loop.

On a very cold night, Tuesday, December 19,1905, Engine Company 40 responded to a 3-11 alarm fire at 1309-11 North Wicker Park Avenue, northwest of the "Loop". Lieutenant Bassett reported to Chief Campion, who ordered him to lead out a hose line to the east side of the burning three story brick warehouse.

As the long lead out began the hose wagon moved through the snow and ice toward the engine company that was next to the hydrant. Lt. Bassett helped straighten the hose line, and he had the pipe and was walking toward the rear of the lot next door of the fire building. All of a sudden there was an unusual cracking noise, and instantly the whole east wall of the burning building came crashing down with a deafening sound. Lt. Henry Bassett was instantly killed and several firemen were inquired by the falling bricks.

That morning I was called by my friend, Captain Alex Lannon, and when he told me the news about Lieutenant Henry Bassett I was in disbelief. It couldn't be, I thought. I went directly over to Engine 50's firehouse, and not until I heard it from Captain Lannon did I really know the story was true. Lieutenant Henry Bassett, President of the Firemen's Association, was killed in the line of duty. On Friday, December 21, 1905, if you are a Firemen in Chicago, there was only two places that you could be that morning; in the firehouse or at the funeral of Lieutenant Henry Bassett.

The two platoon system is still working well, but the city council was not pleased because it would cost the taxpayers more money for the change in the firemen's hours. The purpose of the two platoon system was to give firemen a better opportunity to spend a larger portion of their time with their families. By means of increased revenues from Saloon licenses in 1906, the budget was met. Officers, firemen, and many friends of Henry vowed to keep the Firemen's Association moving forward.

I was asked to take Henry's place in the Association, but I declined because of my age, but this Association of young men began taking up many of the ideas of Henry Bassett.

Changes on the Fire Department continued and Mayor Dunne was looking in all directions to somehow cut the budget. The new license tax that was voted in was not enough to cover the extra men that would need to be hired on the Fire Department. The Mayor of Chicago, Edward Dunne, was good to the Fire Department. For most requests, Mayor Dunne was considered to be a reformer and an honest politician when corruption in Chicago politics was rampant. Chief Campion, now in charge of the Chicago Fire Department continued his expansion plans.

Chief Campion showed the Mayor his plans for building six new firehouses and remodeling eleven firehouses, and the request to purchase four new steam engines and two trucks.

The Mayor was impressed with the Chief's expansion plans for the Department, except for the purchase of the steam engines. In the request it only showed one company in the bidding, The American Engine Company. Mayor Dunne wanted steam engines to be bid on from all over the country, not just this formed company of many builders. The American Engine Company's purpose was to dominate the fire apparatus industry in America by eliminating all the competition. Mayor Dunne did not like this.

Chief Campion explained to the Mayor that a request for a bid was only sent to The American Engine Company because this was the only company who knew the specifications on Chicago engines. The Mayor ordered Chief Campion to draw up new specifications that included all American manufacturers of steam engines. It was much more competitive and more honest and above board.

Many months later, the new set of specifications were sent to the other steam engine companies. However, the specifications were not sent to the William S. Nott Steam Engine Company from Minneapolis, Minnesota. The Mayor ordered Chief Campion to his office and asked him how many Nott Universal steam engines are in service. The Mayor did his homework and found out that William Nott, a Chicago raised boy, moved to Minnesota and began manufacturing steam engines. This steam engine that W.S. Nott builds comes with a five year guarantee and is offered for $3,700.

Heavy and angry words were being fired back and forth about who is better qualified to purchase fire engines, the chief of the department, or the mayor. Mayor Dunne told Chief Campion that his job was to follow the specific order that he was given and he did not. Every company that built steam engines was to be given the opportunity to submit a bid for the new steam engines. So, as a result, the Mayor requested Campion's letter of resignation.

The news shocked the firemen. Mayor Dunne fired the Chief of the Brigade for insubordination. The real shocker was when the Mayor appointed as Fire Marshal, Captain John McDonough of Engine 1. However, the Chicago City Council did not approve of the Mayor's harsh decision to appoint a captain to the highest position on the Fire Department. As a result, Captain John McDonough's appointment was denied, and after some forty-three days in office he returned to Engine 1 on the morning of July 9, 1906.

James Horan
Fire Marshal and Chief of Brigade 1906-1910

Mayor Dunne wasted no time at all in choosing the next man to lead the Chicago Fire Department. Chief James Horan was the right man for the job of Chief of the Brigade. Horan was appointed on July 9, 1906. Charles Seyferlich became the 1st Assistant Fire Marshal, William Burroughs became 2nd Assistant Fire Marshal, and Thomas O'Connor was now acting 3rd Assistant Fire Marshal and the department inspector was now John McDonnell. This was Chief James Horan's chosen few who he trusted to carry out his plans for the Chicago Fire Department. The Fire Department, in 1906 was comprised of 108 steam engines, 31 hook and ladders, one water tower, and 15 chemical engines. There were four fire boats in service; The Denis Swenie, The Michael W. Conway, The Chicago, and The Illinois.

The first action of Chief Horan was to inspect each and every firehouse, along with the chief of that battalion, and Assistant Chief Fire Marshals. Notes were taken about the care of the company journal, apparatus, horses, tools and the men. Everything about company quarters was examined no matter if conditions were good, bad or indifferent. Everything was looked over, and an entry was made in company journals. After meeting with his chief officers about the over all condition of the Chicago Fire Department, Chief Horan then reported to the Mayor and the City Council. The Fire Chief was well respected by all Aldermen. It was a well-known fact that the Chicago Fire Department had not been running very well for many years. Chief Horan is just what is needed to rebuild the morale and the great pride of the fire department. In order to take a job of the Chief of the Brigade, you need to be a big man, and not just in size. Chief Horan was a big man about six-foot four inches to be exact, and he weighed in at around 200 pounds. All muscle! He showed great energy in everything he did.

Chief Horan was born in Chicago on May 28, 1859 and his parents emigrated from Limerick, Ireland. In 1881 James Horan began his fire career as a "water boy" and in no time, he was promoted to pipe man when he began to show his stuff. By the year 1886 Horan was a lieutenant and in two short years, he was the Captain of Hook and Ladder 6 at 117 North Franklin Street. The fire department was Horan's life. On July 1, 1893 he was promoted to the Chief of the 1st Battalion.

Chief Horan was for all practical purposes a natural born leader. He would never send his men into a situation that he himself wouldn't go into first, and there were many of those situations. He was called "Big Jim" by many because he was very well liked. Not only did the Mayor like him, so did the City Council members, department heads, prominent business men, and influential people of this city. As the saying goes on the fire department, he hit the floor with his boots on when he took this job.

After securing the support of the members of the City Council he then explained the true condition of the fire department when he took command. Chief Horan laid it out as plainly as he could. "Chicago does not have, in a great part of the city, more than half the protection against fire it ought to have. The City of Chicago now has about 190 square miles and there are 108 engines and 31 truck companies the chief continued. Two-fifth of this fire protection is stationed in the factory and business districts, and these districts cover a relatively small part of the total area of the city," the chief said, "The citizens of Chicago have had the opportunities to see firemen work, and respond with great efficiency. It astonishes many people to see how fast the fire department responds to and extinguishes fires. In many cases they think, it is only a small fire, and the firemen will be here in a minute to put it out. So the bottom line," the chief said, "is that the physical facilities and equipment to fight fires are inadequate, and these defects should be remedied as soon as possible."

After convincing Mayor Dunne and the City Council to increase the Chicago Fire Department budget, Chief Horan then began planning how he would wisely spend the new money. Number one on his agenda was to add one fireman to each fire company in the city. By adding this extra fireman, this would allow firemen and officers one day, or 24 consecutive hours off, every sixth working day. The next item on Chief Horan's list was to give a 10% salary increase, and his critics said he was playing favoritism with tax money. Chief Horan's reply was, "Just wait and see." He told the insurance companies. "With the extra manpower and better paid firemen, they will be rested and perform their jobs much better and with greater efficiency."

In Chief Horan's first months in office, he began the major project of remodeling and repairing fire houses. Twenty five firehouses were made with better and healthier living quarters and a little more comfortable. Chiefs Burroughs, was one of the best and most knowledgeable persons, when it came to fire apparatus. It was requested by him that the city purchase ten new steam engines, twenty-five new hose wagons and one new hook and ladder truck, along with thousands of feet of new fire hose. On the construction end, nine new firehouses were being built. Chief Seyferlich along with Chief Horan kept a careful watch on this construction. Along with all the new things that were happening on the fire department there had to be some justification for what all this money was being spent on.

The firemen and the fire houses were to be inspected daily; all apparatus would be examined carefully by the officer and engineers in the morning and after each fire call. One drill per day was conducted at the Battalion Chiefs discretion, and during the months of May, June, July, August, September and October a full "run out" drill was conducted. Upon receiving the call when the bell rang, firemen and officers from the firehouses bunkroom would slide the pole, hitch the horses, and pull out of the firehouse to the nearest hydrant. Firemen would stretch 300 feet of a 2 1/2" hose with a 1 inch nozzle, and the engineer would generate 100 lbs. of water pressure, and hold it for 15 minutes.

Often times, Chief Horan would show up unannounced to watch the drill. If the drill was not completed to his liking, the fire company was ordered to pick up all the hose and return to the firehouse. Then the same drill was done over and over until the fire company got it right for Chief Horan. Everything that Horan was doing with all this training and fast push outs, was all about saving lives and property. Chief Horan's thinking was when the alarm is called in; the firemen will push out fast from the firehouse and get to the scene while the fire is small. If they have to lead out fire hose they can do it in a faster time. The idea is to save insurance companies money and it was beginning to work and work well!

Chief Horan was admired and respected by his men, and he was always tempting the newest of his 1700 firemen to call him Jim. If they made that mistake, the chief would come down on them like a ton of bricks! There were a few that called him "Jim" or "Big Jim", but only a very few close friends or firemen. The chief was a stern disciplinarian and a stickler for detail. If a rule was broken and somehow he found out about the matter, it would be dealt with, and if needed, full punishment would be administered.

In the twenty-five years of being a firemen on this job, the one thing that bothered Horan the most was the fact that all of the horses on the Chicago Fire Department had to continually wear their harnesses 24-hours a day. It was a rule, to ensure a fast push out to a fire. Well that was going to end because 500 Kennedy Hanging Harness sets were installed in all the firehouses, which would decrease the push out time considerably.

The Kennedy Hanging Harnesses is a unique invention and Chief Horan liked the invention right away. For a couple of reasons, first a faster push-out; get the firemen to the fire earlier. But second, it was with great pleasure to Chief Horan to get those heavy harnesses and collars off the horses. The Hanging Harness works the instant the alarm begins to ring. The horses push open their stall door and take their position in the front of the engine, truck, or hose wagon.

The driver of the rig climbs up into his seat; the harness is always suspended from the ceiling above the horses. The driver grabs hold of the reins, the tension loosens the springs and the harness then drops down on the horses. The firemen then snaps the collar around the horse's neck and an automatic weight attached to the little pulleys in the ceiling carrying the framework of the hanger up overhead, out of the way. In about one minute from the first sounds of the alarm, the fire company will be out the door and on their way to the fire.

With a lot of assistance from Chief Burroughs all the horses were evaluated, some for age, injuries, and sickness. Chief Horan found out that there were not enough horses in reserve and made a purchase of 476 horses out of a compliment of 760 horses.

Today I had to pick up supplies for my wagon business, at Archer Road and Western Avenue. As I pulled in, I spied an old friend of mine, Joe Mackey, standing alongside his buggy. Right away I yelled, "Hey, Joe," and Mackey looked up with a smile. I pulled up next to him, got down keeping a hold or the reins and we shook hands. "Norm", he said, "you look good for an old retired horse". "What are you guys doing here?" I asked. "The city is buying a lot of, or I should say, that Chief Horan is buying a lot of horses for the job because with some of these older horses' pulling days are over."

With that, Chief Horan saw me through the window, he stood up and left the man who was selling him the horses. Out the side door of the building the chief came down the few stairs and shook my hand, and gave me an embrace. "Well how are you, Norm," the chief said. "Where have you been keeping yourself?" I told the Chief that Nancy and I are still involved with the widows and orphans and also the Firemen's Association, plus my wagon business keeps me in "beer money".

I told me that since Chief Horan has taken control of the department, the firemen are all in good moods and their just happy to come to work. "They are in good moods, Norm," the Chief said, "because they got a 10% raise and twenty-four hours off. A fireman is making a good living, a little over $1,255 a year now and that's good money, Norman Doolan" the chief said, "But it's not a gift. They are going to work their asses off for it!" Norm said.

"I want results, Norm," the chief said. "Faster push-outs, and water on the fire as soon as possible. The new horses will help the response time, there are some nags out there, and they need to be replaced and put out to posture."

"Norm," the chief went on, "I have been drilling and timing them, and then drilling them again. It has been hard on them, but it's paying off. As a matter of fact there is a truck company on the east side that is getting out in just less than a minute." "What truck?" I asked. "Truck 11. A good bunch of young, full of piss and vinegar guys under the direction of Lieutenant Herman Brandenburg," he said.

"Hey "Big Jim" I said. "Isn't that kid ,Moriarity, whose brother is a

109

baseball player on Truck 11"? "Yeah, that is him, and not only does he have one brother, he has two that play professional baseball. The one brother, Billy," the chief said, "He almost made the White Sox. The other brother George, he plays for the Detroit Tigers."

"The Chicago White Sox are going all the way, Norm," the Chief said as he climbed up into his buggy. "You bet they are," I replied? The chief said, "This will be my last buggy, Norm." "Why is that boss?" I asked. "Because, I am on my way to purchase a brand new, 1906 two-cylinder Buick and give the horse a break. I'll see you later, Norm," the Chief said as he pulled away. I waved my hand and thought to myself; this guy Horan is a natural leader with a plan.

Chief Horan had a plan on how to change fire fighting in Chicago by increasing the manpower, giving essential time off for resting, and a 10% salary increase. In less than a year, Horan and his assistant chiefs cleaned up and painted the inside walls and ceilings of fire houses. All windows were repaired or replaced. They even got new iron beds with springs and hair mattresses. They remodeled twenty firehouses

I thought back to the old days, we had nothing but engines, horses and hoses. All combination engines were equipped with a hose wagon, and they purchased one hundred forty thousand feet of 2 ½ inch and 3 inch fire hose. With all the administration work, construction and training of Chief Horan, he still responds to fires throughout the city. If Chief Horan saw smoke, he would tell his driver, Joe Mackey, let's get a little closer and as they got a little closer to the plume of smoke, he would observe and if the smoke got lighter that would mean they're got water on the fire. They chief would say turn around and they would go back to what they were doing before they saw smoke.

In City Hall, Chief Horan met with his staff, and was very pleased with how the training and drilling has turned the fire department around. When the training began there were plenty of firemen who didn't know some of the basics of fire fighting. As the meeting continued Chief Seyferlich gave an outstanding report of the nine new firehouses that are under construction, and Chief Horan was very pleased.

Chief Horan was happy because the fire department was running well, almost to his liking. He was also happy because he was going to the first game of the World Series; The Chicago White Sox against the Chicago Cubs. All of Chicago was excited about the World Series in Chicago, with both the Cubs and Sox playing each other. How much more exciting could baseball get?

The series is now the Sox two wins and the Cubs one win. I met up with my boyhood friends. We belong to a club called "the Bulls" and have been meeting for over thirty years. The founding member of the Bulls was a grammar school friend, Marty Ryan, a Chicago Police Officer, who passed away a few years ago.

We still meet on Thursday nights, every other week. Mike, Jim, Ed, John, and Tom are Sox fans and Jimmy D. is a Cubs fan. We meet in a pub on Western Avenue called McNally's. We crowd around the radio to listen to the World Series, and drink Topaz Beer.

Chief Horan is going to be sitting at the game with two of his boyhood friends, Charles Comisky who happens to own the Chicago White Sox, and Fred Busse who is running for Mayor against Mayor Dunne. Jim Horan did not get into politics, and especially not this race. Fred Busse was an everyday friend since they were kids, but Mayor Dunne was the person who chose Horan to be the Chief of the Brigade, so Chief Horan was staying neutral.

The White Sox have a good team, because Charles Comisky built his team on pitching and Ed Walsh who could pitch four hundred innings per season. The Chicago Cubs also had a good team, and won over one hundred sixteen regular season games. Chief Horan was unable to attend all the World Series games between the Sox and the Cubs, but as a result of the 1906 season the Chicago White Sox won the pennant and their first World Series in a stunning upset over the Chicago Cubs. The White Sox were dubbed in the newspaper as the "hitless wonders" for having the lowest team batting averages, but never the less, took the series in six games.

Horan loved the game of baseball so much he would often times make it a point to visit hook and ladder 11's firehouse. Al Moriarty and his brothers would talk baseball all evening with the chief. By the time that the New Year 1907 rolled around, the fire department was running just the way Chief Horan liked. But the chief still had some "pet" projects to do, like standardizing the equipment of the Chicago Fire Department.

There were no standards on any of the Chicago Fire Department equipment, everything was made by different companies and everything was different sizes. Chief Horan changed that and established standard engines and hose wagon sizes. All the pumps and suction fittings would now be interchangeable so wheel sizes and axles were now the same.

Horan's plans to lower the total fire losses by thirty percent were working. He showed prominent businessman and influential people in the insurance industry that we can "put them out" efficiently. He told them if you want the Chicago Fire Department to stop these large fire losses; then give me the men and the equipment, and I'll put the fires out.

Water was Chief Horan's menace. Before him it was Chief Campion's menace and before him it was Chief Musham's menace. They all urged the City Council to install a high water pressure system in the business district, and in the union stockyards. Time after time, they refused because of the inadequate fourth city charter that dates back to 1872. Under the state constitution, the legislative Branch has been prevented from passing any special laws. For years that body had been obliged to resort to the makeshift patchwork of passing general laws for cities over 100,000 in order to meet the growing needs of Chicago. While there were many fires in Chicago, no single loss was only more than one-hundred thousand dollars, because Chief Horan's plan was working.

On the last Tuesday of February, 1907 Chicago elected its first republican mayor in ten years. Fred A. Busse won the popular vote over Mayor Dunne. Fred Busse was one of Chief Horan's closest friends, and although Mayor Dunne appointed him Chief of the Brigade, Horan was supporting his long-time friend.

Chief Horan continued his fast pace, and with Assistant Chief Burrough's projections of where the next fire companies should be organized and when Chief Burrough informed the Chief of the Brigade that the west side and the north side were now in the most need of fire companies.

On a Sunday afternoon, May 5, 1907, a fire occurred in a box factory located at forty-first and Ashland Avenue, in the northwest section of the Chicago Stockyards. When Engine Company 53 arrived on the scene, there was heavy smoke emanating from the windows on the east side of the eighth floor.

Chief Burrough requested a 3-11 alarm immediately, because of the water pressure in the small inadequate water mains of the stockyards. The fire was very stubborn to extinguish. There were piles of cardboard stacked boxes, and it took many firemen who fought into the wee hours of the evening before Chief Horan struck out the fire; because the over hauling of all that cardboard took hours. There was a lot of damage to the structure, but it was not a total loss, due to the hard work of the Chicago Fire Department.

In June and July of 1907 Truck Company 32 and Engine Company 109 were organized on the west side located at the 1107 South Whipple Avenue, it was a proud day for all newly assigned firemen.

In September of 1907, Engine Company 110 was organized up north in the 13th Battalion, and the next month Engine Company 112 was also added to the 13th Battalion. Engine Company 111 was organized on October 31,

1907 along with Engine Companies 113 and 114. All in all, the year of 1907 was very successful for the Chicago Fire Department. Training was at an all time high; there were many fires, but only a few extra alarm fires with small losses compared to previous years.

Chief Horan tried in every way he could to convince the City Council to help him install the high pressure system within the business district where there are many fires. Chief Seyferlich suggested to Horan to give the City Council an estimate for the water mains needed to be installed in the business district, and then they will have some idea about how much it might cost to install a high pressure water system.

Chief Seyferlich recalled that Chief Musham tried to convince the City Council with an estimate of a sixteen inch pipeline from the river south to VanBuren, on all the North and South streets in the business district. Chief Horan liked the idea and ordered Seyferlich to begin working on the estimate, as soon as possible. Chief Horan instructed Chief Seyferlich to concentrate only in the business district in the downtown area, and not the stockyard district. Horan was sure that he will not get a high pressure system in the stockyards it if meant that the millionaire meat barons had to come up with any money.

The railroads contributed most of the money needed to build the yards. The meat magnates chose the yards because they were then outside the city limits, and therefore, avoided paying municipal taxes. This is how the owners of the meat packing companies became millionaires, since they did not have their businesses located within the city limits! Also, they had their own water supply, and all the fires within the Stockyards were extinguished by the Chicago Fire Department.

There is a makeshift system of wells and reservoirs in the stock yards. The meat packers said that this water system was better than the city of Chicago's but the firemen knew that it wasn't. Half of the time the system was shut down because of some problem or another. Chief Horan knew that the Aldermen of this city were wining and dining with the meat barons. They were expecting gifts and campaign contributions for their votes for things that were pertaining to the stockyards like the high pressure water system.

These were the wealthiest people in Chicago, probably in the nation. Armor, Swift, and the Nelson Morris meat barons, who last year slaughtered five million hogs, two million cattle, and three million sheep. They employ thirty-thousand people, who work in the most deplorable, filthy, and dangerous conditions.

In total, the workers earned twenty-three million dollars in wages, and the gross product generated in the stockyards in 1906, was three hundred twenty-five million dollars for the meat barons. This is big money, and it can change or not change things in this city, but, Big Jim Horan knew how to handle these meat barons, or so he thought.

The population is spreading out to the west of the city, and vacant lots are being rapidly filled up. Chief Horan's next big move was to organize the 18th Battalion, and getting the much needed fire protection to these people who live in Chicago's western district. The boundary lines for this new battalion will be Kedzie Avenue on the east, the city limits on the west, Division Street on the north, and Sixteenth Street on the south. The new 18th Battalion Chief is Eugene Sweeny, a very good friend of mine from years ago.

The following fire companies made up the 18th Battalion: Engine Companies 67, 77, 85, 95, 113, and hook & ladder Companies 26 and 29. The chief's headquarters will be in hook & ladder 26's fire house, located at 3985 West Wilcox Street. Chief Horan was very proud of this new fire battalion on the west side. It filled a big void and the citizens finally have fire protection that was sorely needed on the west side of Chicago.

August 3, 1908 began as another hot dry day in Chicago, with no rain in the forecast. In fact there had been no rain in this region for over two and a half months! When I kick the ground, dust would blow out from the dry ground. Chicago firemen were well aware of the dry conditions. Alarms were up some fifty percent, and people were getting a little edgy. I didn't like it either, because it would remind me of how dry it was just before the great Chicago fire.

I will remember this day for years to come. The Burlington railroad yards are located just a short distance southwest of the downtown business district. The yard stretches about one half mile long and about one quarter mile wide, and is located on the east side of Canal Street. There is a very large freight house of the Burlington Railroad near Canal Street and about Sixteenth Street. Just after the lunch hour, as some men were finishing their lunches, someone accidentally flipped a lit cigarette amongst some chemicals that were being shipped over to the powder factory.

Instantly, there were several loud explosions heard, then the flames shot upward and around the outside walls of the structure. Many more explosions occurred very rapidly and they were very loud. The Burlington freight house was full of stock to the point of overflowing because two large freighters had just finished unloading. The fire rapidly traveled upward to the roof and across the wood shingles. Within minutes the whole freight house was engulfed in flames.

The Burlington freight house was located between two slips leading from the south branch of the Chicago River. Just to the north of the freight house were two giant grain elevators marked, E & F, and these elevators contained about 700,000 bushels of wheat and about 100,000 bushels of corn. The fire quickly engulfed the two giant grain elevators.

The Chicago Fire Department received a call from an alarm box on Roosevelt Road just before 1:00 pm. When Engine Company 6 pulled out of their firehouse, all they could see was a wall of fire to the east. The grain elevators E&F, both had cupolas on top which are some two hundred feet from the ground. In no time at all, both of the cupolas where belching out heavy smoke. With the hot dry southwest wind, the smoke began to cover the downtown business district in a very short time. I was at Engine Company 61's firehouse, replacing the front bearings on Lieutenant Eddy Danis' wagon. All of the firemen were out on the south lawn next to the firehouse playing horseshoes, there were many tournaments held there.

Suddenly Lieutenant Danis came running out in front, and told me that Engine 61 is responding to the 3-11 & 1 special alarm at 16th and Canal Street. As I looked to the North all you could see was black smoke hundreds of feet in the air. I jumped into my wagon and followed engine 61 to the fire.

Chief Fire Marshal Horan knew this area and how dangerous a fire in this area could become. And, Horan in his 1906 Buick began to respond to the box alarm as fast as the vehicle could travel. He was on the scene within a matter of minutes. Again, water became a big problem for the firemen as the nearest fire hydrant was almost a half a mile away. If the water was a problem, the wind would be a bigger problem, with very strong winds from the southwest and some of the driest conditions in years; again the firemen were at the mercy of the wind. Miles of fire hose is now being stretched to the hydrants in the area, but Chief Horan knew he had to get water from the river or he could have another Chicago Fire on his hands.

The flames were over two hundred feet in the air and the radiant heat from the burning structures became so terrific, the railroad cars began bursting into flames. Chief Horan thought, how can we get these steam engines over all these railroad tracks? A young Lieutenant, Herman Branderberg, from Hook & Ladder Company 11, came up with the idea of taking lumber that is stacked over by the side of the river and building it up high enough that it will be even with the steel tracks. This idea worked real well and Chief Horan yelled out loud and clear, "Let's get to work boys."

So with every available fireman and railroad personnel, they began laying down the lumber. At first, they did a test over three sets of railroad tracks. The test was a little shaky, but once the horses settled down because of the loose wood, it began to work. They continued bridging the tracks with the lumber, one after the next. It was so hot the men needed to be sprayed down with fire hoses, as they got closer to the river. The horses pulling the big engine were covered and wet down before they began the cross over the fifteen sets of railroad tracks. The firemen led the horses by the reins and walked them across the temporary planked roadway. A steady wind was blowing cinders from the southwest, right into the firemen, who were now setting up along the bank of the south branch of the Chicago River. Finally the steam engines began drafting water, and in a short time eighteen engines were dotted along the river bank. I could see that the horses were foaming at the mouths, because there was no water, and the firemen were also very thirsty. I began getting water from the hoses into buckets, water from the city hydrants, but I knew that they would need a lot more water.

We first emptied a hose wagon, and Patrol Company 3 placed tarpaulins inside the wagon and then filled it with water. The firemen slowly moved the water wagon out close enough to carry the water in buckets to the over-heated firemen. The heat was so intense that firemen fell to their knees and crawled toward the fire with hose lines in hand, while other firemen played their streams on them to prevent their fire clothes from bursting into flames.

The first fire boat to arrive at the fire was the Dennis J. Sweenie, and they began shooting hundreds of gallons of water on the inferno from their large five and one half inch nozzles. Next the fireboat "Chicago" arrived and set up on the south end of the fire. Soon after, the fire boat "Illinois" set up in the middle, just to the north of the fireboat Chicago. Chief Horan began to see some progress with the three fire boats and eighteen engine companies all throwing thousands of gallons of water on the two tall grain elevators, E&F. The almost super human bravery of every firemen working at this fire finally began to check the flames.

Only again to have more difficulties, the engines that were pumping at the river bank, began to run low on coal to fuel the engines. The coal supply wagon that was trying to cross the plank trail over the tracks had to unhitch the horses from the wagon because of the extreme heat, the two horses fell down on the tracks, tipping the coal wagon and spilling coal on the ground. Firemen began to carry bags of coal and many carried arms full of coal to the engines that needed the coal to produce steam.

There were insurmountable problems that faced the Chief and his brave firemen, and the next problem was flying embers. As a result of the high winds, cinders and flying blazing, embers began to ignite fires to many structures east of the Burlington Railway yard and as far east as Wabash Avenue. Chief Horan assigned Chief Egan of the first battalion along with the firemen of eight engine companies, two hook & ladder companies, and four chemical engines, to work on extinguishing these fires. The firemen chased the flaming embers up stairways trying to extinguish them before they got out of control.

They traveled up and down the streets east of the fire, Michigan Avenue, Wabash, and State Street, extinguishing fires on roof tops and awnings. One hundred and thirty fires were extinguished in all. The fire was now burning in the railroad yard from the Twelfth Street viaduct all the way south to Sixteenth Street, where the fire had originated. Over one hundred railroad freight cars loaded with goods were now burning.

In the midst of the blinding drift of burning embers, the firemen stood their ground with their Chief at their side. It was only by pure heroism and determination that the fire was checked, because for a short while the Chief of the Brigade thought of the great Chicago fire. Finally there was a brake for the tired firemen. The direction of the wind veered from the southwest to the west. With this change of the wind, the Chicago firemen began controlling the flames from the Burlington railroad yards.

The burning cupolas on top of the grain elevators E&F, began falling forward toward the river along with sections of the walls. As they hit the ground, flames shot out over two hundred feet and set fire to the docks on the east bank of the river. Immediately, the boat's turrets were turned to extinguish the fires. After the collapse of the elevators E&F, the fire raged in the large piles of grain. The engines, fireboats, and firemen worked their streams on the collapsed structures throughout the night. Some time about 3:30 am there was a sudden tremendous explosion that occurred in grain elevator "F" caused by the build up of gases in the heated grain. The explosion blew one of the walls outward that landed on the bow of the fire boat "Illinois" causing great damage. The ropes held the boat to the docks, but not for long, the fire boat "Illinois" sank in twenty feet of water in the south branch of the Chicago River. The firemen from the "Illinois" were rescued from the river unharmed.

The exhausted firemen of Chicago continued to pour water on the ruins of the Burlington Railroad yards for days. Chief Horan informed the press that for some two hours yesterday Chicago again was at the mercy of wind and fire. In closing with the press, Chief Horan stated that he was very proud of the Chicago firemen and the work they did here yesterday. They are the best, and the bravest firemen in this country the Chief informed the press, and he said "I and all of Chicago can and should, be proud of them". The Chicago Tribune praised the Chicago firemen and their brave Chief for probably one of the most heroic feats in the history of the Chicago Fire Department. It was just short of a miracle that none of these brave firemen were killed or seriously injured.

There were some top priorities for Chief Horan after the Burlington yard fire. Number one on that list was to get the fireboat "Illinois" off the bottom of the Chicago River.

Number two on his list was to set up a support system of extra equipment in the case of another conflagration. Two extra hose wagons with one thousand feet of 2 ½ inch hose would be centrally located so they could respond city wide. In the following days, all the engine and truck companies were reloaded with equipment and the fire boat "Illinois" was raised up and off the bottom of the Chicago River and, after some repairs, put back in service. In the following months of 1908 Chief Horan and Chief Seyferlich and Burroughs continued their fast pace of expanding the fire department by building new firehouses and remodeling firehouses in need of refurbishing.

In 1909, the Chicago Fire Department added two more fireboats to the three that were already in service. "The Graeme Stewart" and "The Joseph

Medill" were launched in early spring. At the launching, Chief Horan said, "These powerful floating engines are indispensable nowadays, as we all saw at the Burlington Railroad fire last August. These fireboats can do the work of twelve engines and the volume of water they provide is far more effective than many streams from nozzles of smaller gauge. We will also use these fireboats to supply engines in areas with low water pressure that are in close proximity to the river," the Chief said.

For the second year in a row now, Chief James Horan was invited back to be the keynote speaker at the Chicago Institute of Social Science. The Chief was very humble about himself but he would cause much excitement when it came to speaking about the Chicago Fire Department and his firemen. This year Chief William Burroughs was also invited to attend the affair at the Chicago Institute. However; not to listen but to speak of the many accomplishments of his boss, Chief Horan. Chief Burroughs was not one to over play Chief Horan because he knew the Chief was very humble about himself and he did not like" grand standing".

Everyone took their seats and the first person to be announced to speak was Assistant Chief of the Brigade, Fire Marshal William Burroughs. Chief Horan looked up from his papers and gave Burroughs a look like, what's going on? Chief Burroughs looked at Chief Horan and just shrugged his shoulders and then walked up to the podium.

He began by saying, "My name is Chief William Burroughs, and that he was asked by a Committee to introduce the keynote speaker Chief James Horan. You can not just call out his name and say 'here he is' because there is a lot to tell about Chief Horan. I have known him for over twenty years; we have become great friends and have worked side-by-side in some mighty dangerous situations. James Horan became Chicago firemen at the age of twenty-two, and began as a "water boy". In a very short time he became a "pipeman" and on March 1, 1886, Jim Horan was promoted to Lieutenant. While he was working at a fire located at twenty North Rush Street, Lieutenant Horan was alerted that a young man was trapped on the second floor of the burning building. Lieutenant Horan, without hesitation and without regard for his own personal safety, ran up the stairs into the smoke-filled building. On the second landing, he found a man who was overcome by smoke lying on the floor and picked him up and carried the unconscious man down to safety. It would not be the last rescue Chief Horan would make. While at a 2-11 alarm fire on a cold March evening in 1889, a fireman suddenly lost his balance and fell into the icy cold Chicago River and he was drowning. Instantly, Captain Horan removed his heavy fire coat and boots jumped into the river and pulled the fireman to safety." Chief Burroughs continued, "In 1891 Captain Horan and the fireman of hook & ladder 6 rescued a women and six men who were on the third and forth floors of a burning building at 125 West Washington Street with raised ground ladders. The rescues were viewed by hundreds of people in the downtown area. There were many more rescues by this daring fireman, who thinks more of the men he works with, than he does of himself."

As Chief Horan walked up to the podium he was received a standing ovation. He gave his speech, but did not talk about any of his feats of bravery. He did tell some great stories and was described as one of the best story tellers who spoke with his eyes. On the way back to City Hall, Chief Horan thanked Chief Burroughs for all the nice words of praise, but he said, " next time keep them to yourself".

During the day Chief Horan had a very busy schedule, early meetings then drilling fire companies and overseeing the building of firehouses. There was always some type of social gatherings that he would have to attend and let's not forget, responding to fires. The Chief would drop everything he was doing at the time, and he would respond to larger fire incidents, only to return to his office in City Hall to attend to his paperwork. The only time that he was able to complete any of his work was after everyone had left City Hall for the day, and went home.

At his desk in City Hall, the Chief would work late into the night writing about the newest project he had in mind. His newest one was the Rules and Regulations book that he was trying to finish. He wanted to give each fireman the rules and regulations book on the first of the year in 1911. With the help of his Assistant Fire Marshals, Seyferlich and Burroughs, they put together many rules that will be followed. It was Chief Horan's intention to make this fire department the best of the best and as a semi-military entity, a procedure of Rules and Regulations was imperative.

Chief Horan built a new and modern the Chicago Fire Department with the new firehouses, equipment, engines, trucks and fireboats. He trained these men how to work in this most dangerous profession of firefighting. Now, Chief Horan would give the firemen a set of rules and regulations to follow in the administration of the fire department. If Chief Horan wasn't in his City Hall office, then you might find him in his second office located upstairs of engine 103 at 1459 West Harrison Street. This was the closest to his home at 722 South Ashland Blvd, and an addition was added to this firehouse for his drivers and his 1906 Buick automobile.

As the new year of 1910 rolled in, Assistant Chief Fire Marshal

Seyferlich had finished with the finale estimates for the sixteen inch water mains. It was a big job to figure the amount of pipe in the business district, but that is why Chief Horan assigned it to the "Big Sey", which was Horan's nickname for Chief Fire Marshal Seyferlich. He was a numbers man. Not only did he figure the cost, Chief Seyferlich figured a time line of how long it would take to install this main pipeline. The pipeline was originally figured to be temporarily used for the fireboats, but "Big Sey" figured it differently. When installing this sixteen inch pipe he designed it to be used temporarily for the fireboats. When the high pressure system is installed, these main lines could then be used permanently and there would be no reason to reinstall any more pipelines. Chief Horan was pleased with the estimate, but it would still be a hard sell to the City Council in December. The cost was far less than previously thought, so he thought he would be able to get the approval of the City Council for this expansion of the water system.

Chief Horan spent many hours establishing a special unit within the Chicago Fire Department to inspect structures that stored explosive materials. The main reason why the fire at the Burlington Railroad yard occurred was that some idiot flipped a cigarette. But, why was the combustible explosive powder in that freight house in the first place? If Inspectors made routine critical examinations, and if someone is improperly storing explosive materials then a fire is likely to occur. Inspections might just be able to prevent many fires from occurring.

On October 18, 1910, thirty-nine years after the great Chicago Fire, Chief Horan had his way and the Bureau of Combustibles was established. Offices and fireman began inspecting structures throughout Chicago. Chief Horan called me on the telephone, to see if I was going to attend the meeting for the Benevolent Association. I informed the Chief that I would be there. I have been an officer of the Association since 1900. The Officers and Directors or the Benevolent Association of the paid fire department of Chicago called a meeting once a year. The meeting is held at Engine Company 13's firehouse on the third floor located at 19 North Dearborn. The meeting was called to order and a roll call was taken. Many things were discussed, including the amount of widows and children with on pension. There are sixty-six widows, three destitute firemen, and sixteen children on the pension roll of the association. The yearly amounts that were paid out for benevolent purposes up until September 1910, was $7,530. The Association had on September 15, 1910, a total in cash and securities of $52,011.08.

I asked for the floor and John McDonnell, President of the Benevolent

Association, banged his gavel down. "The association recognizes Norman Doolan" I started by saying, "We have three destitute firemen on the roll. There should not be a destitute firemen person; a person who gave his all while he was a Chicago fireman. Destitute means he has no clothing or food, as officers and members we can not have one our own living like this. We need to give them more," and I sat down.

I got a wink and a nod from Chief Horan, and after the meeting, he came over and said "Norm, you are passionate about helping these guys and that is good," Chief Horan shook my hand and asked me if I was going to Captain Matt Moran's retirement party on December 15th. I replied "I wouldn't miss his party". Chief Horan handed me two tickets for the party and said, "This is for you and Nancy. Will you sit at his table?" and I replied "Absolutely, I would be honored!"

The retirement party honoring Captain Edward Tetzner, Captain Rooney, and Captain Matthew Moran was held on Thursday evening December 15, 1910 at the coliseum located at 1501 South Wabash Avenue. This was definitely a "who's-who" party, and everyone wore their finest. Cocktails were from 6:30 pm to 7:30 pm and the tables were set up throughout, with Battalion Engines and Truck Numbers displayed on the tables.

Truck 11, had their own table because of Captain Matt Moran, who taught them how to be the best truck men on the job. This was an inseparable group and they all had their wives sitting with them. Lieutenant Herman Branderburg, Nick Doyle, Al Moriarty, Pete Powers and Eddie Schonsett had the bragging rights to their being the fastest push outs in the city.

Engine 59 had their own tables because of Ed Tetzner, who called Engine 59 the yards of the stockyards. Captain Pat Collins, Frank Walters, and Billy Weber, George Murawski of Engine 49 and Lieutenant William Sturm of Engine 64 were all at that table.

Captain Dennis Doyle, of Engine 39 sat with Lieutenant James Fitzgerald and George Enthof of Engine 23. Also sitting at that table were Captain Doyle and Thomas Costello of Engine 29. Captain Alexander Lannon of Engine 50 had his gang along with Charles Moore and Nicolas Crane of Truck Company 18. Also sitting at this table was Lieutenant Edward Danis of Engine 61.

After the cocktail hour, everyone was seated and the invocation was given by Father John McNails. In front of the Honorees table was Chief Horan and Chief Burroughs. Nancy and I were excited, and honored to be sitting with the Chiefs of the Fire Brigade.

The food was outstanding; there was polish sausage and sauerkraut, Italian sausage and meatballs, and country fried chicken, with roasted potatoes. Most importantly there was plenty of Topaz beer from Ed Cosgrove's Koller Brewing Company in the stockyards. After dinner, the music played all evening long and the boys mustered up to the bar to tell each other "fire stories".

Chief Horan met me at the bar and said, "I would like to buy you a drink, Norm." The Chief continued, "I would like to thank you, Norm, for getting the water to the horses and firemen at the Burlington Railroad yard fire. It is hard to describe that day; the wind was so hot that once we got one steam engine to begin drafting water from the river, the firemen were so thirsty that they drank the water from the hose water from the river! They had to cool themselves, Norm," the Chief said, "there was no water to drink until you brought the water."

After the fire many of the firemen who were out there and drank the water from the river got sick, real sick, and some even died months later. I told the Chief, "Water was the first thing I thought of because I know what it was like as I remember the fire from October 8, 1871".

A grand time was had by all at the party; any leftover money went to the widows and children's fund. As Chief Horan walked out of the coliseum door, he yelled out, "Be good boys, remember we all have to work in the morning."

Winter began setting in, and the cold wind blows down the shores of Lake Michigan and as the saying goes in Chicago "the hawk is out!" People ran in and out of the stores getting ready for Christmas. Chief Horan's wife made plans with the local photographer to have the children's photographs taken so they can give them to their father for Christmas.

Firemen all over the department began making plans to trade time in order to be off on Christmas. Lieutenant James Fitzgerald of Engine Company 23 was making plans at St. Patrick's Roman Catholic Church where he would be married on Christmas Eve. The Moriarty boys were returning home to be with their brother Al, for a special Christmas dinner at Mom's house.

Christmas time in Chicago was a magical time of the year. Chief Horan continued his drive to convince the City Council that with a high pressure water system installed in the downtown business district, it would not only reduce the cost of fire losses, but it would save lives. In a meeting with Chief Seyferlich and Burroughs, Chief Horan went over the numbers and the speech he prepared to give to the City Council.

Since the estimate that Chief Seyferlich prepared was only for the business district, somehow, Chief Horan had to get the same message to the owners of the meat companies in the stockyards about the importance of a high pressure to protect the stockyards. In the case of the downtown business district, the tax payers would have to pay for the system. The meat companies in the stockyards were in more danger than the business district because the buildings were very large and the water system in the yards is turned off at night because of freezing temperatures in cold weather. The cost for the system to be installed in the stockyards would be funded by the meat packing companies.

Chief Horan was well known by the companies in the stockyards, because of their many fires. So he wrote a strongly worded letter to them and asked for their help. The letter starts by saying, " would you kindly advise me if your company would be interested in installing an up-to-date high pressure water system in packing town?" (as the stockyards were called)

The letter went on, the Fire Marshals interest in the matter lies in the fact that every fire of any consequence in the yards district may call out twenty to thirty engines. With all the engines working on the fire in the stockyards, this leaves the entire fire district without any fire companies. Kindly advise me if your company would care to go into this matter. The letter was signed: James Horan Fire Marshal, Chief of Brigade Chicago Fire Department.

On Monday morning December 16, 1910, Chief Horan and First Assistant Fire Marshal Seyferlich and his second Assistant Fire Marshal Burroughs dressed in their class "A" uniform and stood before the City Council. I made my way into the meeting and stood in the back of the chamber. Chief Horan began the presentation of his life, in an effort to convince the Council to vote for the high pressure system in the business district. He started out by showing the Alderman how this system would work.

A sixteen inch pipeline would be installed forty-two inches below the surface of the street. At first our plan was to install a temporary pipeline, but Chief Seyferlich showed us that to install a permanent pipeline would cost no more than the temporary one. These pipelines would be installed in the north and south streets of the loop from Michigan Avenue on the east and Franklin Street on the west. The pipelines would run from the Chicago River back on the north end to Van Buren Street on the south end.

Chief Horan continued, "When a fire occurs in the business district the fireboats will connect their hose lines to the new sixteen inch pipeline and provide positive pressure to that particular pipeline. This action will be able to deliver enough water to supply ten steam engines easily. The best part of this new pipeline is that it will be permanently installed and ready to be used when the high pressure system is installed.

Chief Horan continued talking but they were not all listening to him. He said, "Chief Seyferlich completed an exhaustive amount of work estimating the cost of this project and creating a time line from the start of the project to the finish." The Mayor thanked Chief Horan and his assistants for a great presentation and said they will now take it to the appropriate City Council to committee.

I spoke with Chief Horan after the City Council meeting and told him that his presentation went well. He said, "Norm, did you see them, some were dozing off". "But most of them were listening," I said. "Thanks, Norm, all we can do is wait and see," the chief said.

Well we did not have to wait long to get the results. The City Council members again voted down Chief Horan's proposal for the high pressure water system in the loop. The main reason that the water system was turned down was they said, lack of money, of course.

That is what they always say, but Chief Horan thought differently and he took it personal. Later that night a fire occurred in a wooden two-story house at 4414 South Cottage Grove on the south east side of the city. Upon the arrival of the still alarm fire companies, Engine 45 and hook & ladder 15, there was a very heavy fire and smoke condition.

The very first fire hydrant was frozen and hoses had to be stretched over five hundred feet. Hook & ladder 15 made several rescues and by the time water was put on the fire there were two more structures burning. Chief Burroughs requested a 2-11 alarm and that gave him an additional five more engine companies and also Chief Horan. The temperature was eight degrees above zero, and ice was everywhere. The streets were frozen, engines were frozen and the firemen were frozen. It wasn't until early morning that the fire was under control. It was found out later, that a mother and her two-year old son died in the fire. Chief Horan was mad as hell "Water, water" it was always about water," he yelled.

That next morning on December 21, 1910 the committee that just voted down the high pressure water system was meeting at City Hall. Chief Horan made an abrupt entrance into the subcommittee meeting. One of the councilmen stood up and said, "Excuse me, Chief," but before he could finish, Chief Horan said "No, excuse me" he was very gruff and began speaking.

"We now have steam engines," he said, "and these engines are intended to throw out, at any time, eight streams of water-- four from each side. Now listen up boys. This is the point, if there is a sufficient water supply these engines with eight hose lines will douse any fire," he yelled.

"Listen here, Chief, our hands are tied with high pressure water system,' the councilmen stated. Out loud ,Chief Horan said, "your hands are tied, how can you be so obtuse? I am out here in the streets of this city with the bravest firemen in this country and you can't make a decision, shame on you!" Chief Horan exclaimed. The Chief continued "I have rebuilt the Chicago Fire Department from top to bottom; we have saved many lives, as I said I would. But this is not enough; you continue to hide behind that fake curtain using the act of 1872".

Chief Horan continued to speak "when are you going to stand up like men and amend this act that was enacted some thirty-eight years ago. Things have changed and at that time the act was okay, but now you need to amend it, so we can tap into that 22,000 square mile lake that sits on our doorstep. It is a little too late for the mother and her son who died last night in a fire. However, it may help many other people in this city". Chief Horan turned and walked out of the meeting.

The Stockyards Fire
December 22, 1910

Engine 59 was located at 826 West Exchange Avenue just outside of the stockyards stone gate. The third watch at Engine 59 had begun; one fireman will stand watch for two hours throughout the night to be ready to receive a fire call. Bill Weber is the driver of Engine 59 and he starts his watch by stoking up the fires in the two cast iron stoves on the apparatus floor.

Even though the fire house felt warm, young Billy Weber could feel the cold air oozing through the large front doors of the firehouse. It is Thursday, December 22, 1910, the first full day of winter, he thought to himself. But, all he could think of was his brand new home that he just moved into with his wife and three children last Saturday. With Christmas just three days away, he took the three letters his kids wrote to Santa and he would go shopping when he got off work this morning.

After signing his name and the time he started his watch into the company journal, he made his way back to the stables in the rear of the firehouse to check on the horses. Bill Weber was fond of the horses, and they were fond of him because he was the driver of this steam engine. He gave them the commands when they were hitched and going out in the street.

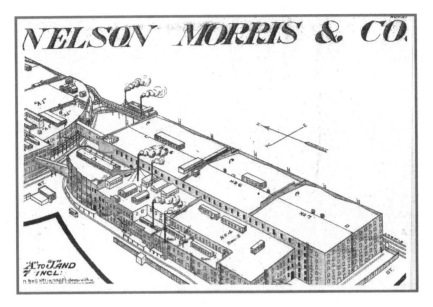

Simultaneously, while Bill Weber was tending to his duties in the firehouse, the night watchman Paul Leska of the Nelson-Morris meat packing company was making his rounds on the exterior of the plant. As he made his way around the corner of 44th and Loomis Street, Leska could smell smoke. He began walking north along the railroad tracks that ran down Loomis Street, when suddenly he saw smoke coming out between the boxcars that were lined up in front of the meat packing warehouse 7. Leska crawled between the boxcars and pulled himself up onto the loading dock platform. He could see heavy black smoke pouring out of a service door entrance.

He opened the door and made his way inside through the smoke, and that was when he discovered that fire was issuing up a stairway that lead down to the basement hide room. The smoke and heat drove him back; he stumbled and fell while escaping. Out in the dark smoky dock area, Leska ran north down the enclosed platform to the adjourning building warehouse 6, where he found an A.D.T. (American District Telegraph) fire alarm. Immediately Leska pulled the A.D.T. snap box fire alarm that instantly transmitted the alarm to the Englewood Fire Alarm Office at 4:09 am

Bill Weber was tending to the horses in the rear stables of engine 59, when suddenly the alarm began to ring in the front of the firehouse. Bill Weber, without hesitation, began to run toward the front of the firehouse. All the time he was listening and counting the number of bells. Box 2162 was being received; that is our box he thought as the second round of bells began ringing Box 2162 again. Weber hooked up at the board for the address, and at the same time he pressed down firmly on the red button. All the bells in the firehouse began ringing,. "43rd and Loomis!" he yelled out.

The adrenaline began to flow in all the firemen as they awakened and started sliding down the brass fire poles to the ground floor. Within one minute the harnesses were dropped down as the horses took their place and the firemen buckled the hitches to the horses. Billy Weber grabbed hold of the reins as the big doors of the firehouse swung open, and they began pulling out onto Exchange Avenue.

In the Union Stockyards there were two firehouses, Engine 53 located at 40th and Packers Avenue and Engine Company 59 located at 826 West Exchange Avenue just outside the stone gate leading into the stockyards. Both firehouses were equipped with an A.D.T. fire alarm system along with the Chicago fire alarm system.

These two engine companies had a jump on the other fire companies that were responding to 43rd and Loomis Street because they were dispatched by the Englewood Fire Alarm Office. As Engine 59 passed through the stockyard gate, Captain Patrick Collins said to Bill Weber, "Boy it is cold out this morning?" "Ya, ya, ya," Bill yelled to the horses as they raced to the fire.

Box 2162 was sent out on registers city wide and the location given was at 43rd and Loomis Street. The engine companies assigned to box 2162 were 39, 49, 52, 53, and Engine 59. These engines were followed by Hook & Ladder Companies 18 and 33, insurance patrol 4, several hose wagons, Battalion Chief Martin Lacey of the 11th Battalion, and 2nd Assistant Fire Marshall William Burroughs also responded.

Engine Company 53 was the first company to arrive on the scene and they noted heavy smoke condition. The wind was blowing out of the southeast at about five miles per hour. The night watchman, Paul Leska, met the arriving fireman and informed them that the fire was in the basement of the Nelson-Morris Meat Packing Plant 7. Once up on the platform that ran along in front of all of the structures, firemen could see smoke emanating from the service door entrance of beef plant building 7. "We need to lead-out the hose from 43rd Street," Captain Collins said.

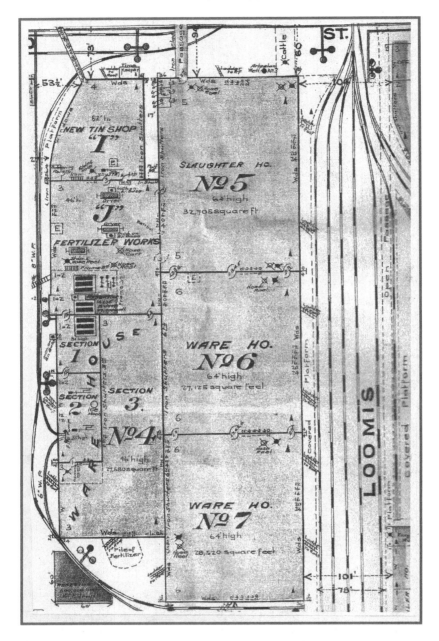

The warehouse that was on fire, was a six-story brick structure with approximate outside dimensions of 300' x 125' x 64'. Warehouse 7 was a solid brick building without any windows. There were a row of iron shutters just above the dock platform. This platform was about fifteen feet deep and ran the length of the building. A row of sliding freight doors faced the platform and they ran the width of the building. The sliding doors are barred and locked from the inside. On the outside of the platform, about fifteen feet across the dock, are a line of box cars of the Chicago Junction Railroad. Overhead, there is an old wooden canopy that was attached to the building that covered the platform. The canopy was rotted in many places and extended just over the railroad box cars to protect the workers from the weather elements while loading refrigerated boxcars.

Engine 53 and Engine 59 led out their hose lines from 43rd Street that was over five hundred feet away. Engine 53 lead their line down Loomis Street over the railroad tracks of the Chicago Junction Railroad. The firemen weaved the hoses between the refrigerated boxcars, up onto the dock where the fire and smoke was issuing from the service entrance door.

Engine 59 led out their line down the platform from 43rd Street, where the steam engine was on a hydrant. But, both engines had to wait for their water, because in the stockyards, the water main that was to feed the fire hydrant was shut down to avoid freezing! Firemen had to force entry by chopping open the door of the head house to open the valves that fed the hydrants.

Chief Martin Lacey and Fire Marshal Burroughs arrived and began to size this one up because this Chief had a lot of experience and knowledge of fire tactics utilized in combating fires in the stockyards. Chief Lacey yelled up to the firemen on the dock, asking if there is any other way to attack this fire than from this loading dock. Captain Lannon of Engine Company 50 informed the Chief that this warehouse was like a fortress, there are no windows or doors, other than the sliding freight doors.

With a large amount of smoke pushing out from under the canopy, Chief Burroughs ordered the firemen of Truck Company 18 to chop a section of the door so they could get a hose stream through. It took over ten minutes to finally get water to the nozzles! Arriving engine companies were leading their lines down the railroad tracks on Loomis Street and up between boxcars toward the dock.

The truckmen labored heavily to chop through the thick freight doors. But once open, the firemen could now see the red glow of the fire. The firemen went down on a knee, because of the smoke and heat that rolled out of that small opening that was made by Truck 18. Now with this canopy over the platform and the railroad boxcars at their back it was like a small enclosure. The firemen struggled to move inward toward the fire, but held their positions on the platform concentrating their hose streams on the fire. After a third hose line was charged on the fire, the pressure in all three of the lines dropped. In order to get water pressure back up arriving engines had to relay water from a great distance, or as it is known in the fire service, "Going in Line".

After fighting the blaze for over thirty minutes, Chief Lacy informed Chief Burroughs that the fire was advancing and how water pressure and limited access to the burning structure was now hindering the firemen on the platform. At this time, the Chief ordered his driver to request a 4-11 alarm. The Chief's driver returned to the alarm box at the corner of 43rd and Loomis. Inside the box is a "Morris Code Type Key" to alert the Fire Alarm Office. The driver would tap erratically many times on the key, meaning that an extra alarm would follow.

The code of signals for an extra alarm fire is as follows, the Chief driver would tap out to the Englewood Fire Alarm Office (F.O.A.) at 4:41 am.

2-1-1	2-1-1	2-1-1	1-2-3
Englewood F.A.O.	Englewood F.A.O	Englewood F.A.O.	2nd Asst. Chief.

Fire alarm operators answer. 2-1-1 Englewood meaning

(For the sender to go ahead with the message).

2162	2162	4-11	1-2-3
Box	Box	Size of Alarm	Chiefs Signature

Fire Alarm Operators Answer ... 1-1 Ok message received

The alarm is sent out city wide to all fire stations

2162 ..... 2162 4-11.... 1-2-3 2162

The 4-11 alarm was to notify the alarm office that all fire companies on box 2162 were needed now. If special alarms were needed the Chief will notify the alarm office at that time.

At Engine Company 103's Firehouse, where Chief Horan's automobile is kept, Lieutenant Joe Mackey, Chief Horan's driver was alerted of the 4-11 alarm. On a 4-11 alarm, the Chief of the Brigade always will respond to a fire in the stockyards. Without hesitation, Joe Mackey, woke up William Moore and they pulled out of the firehouse, located at 1459 West Harrison Street.

While Joe Mackey and William Moore were responding to the Chief Horan's home, the Fire Alarm Office called him on the telephone and informed him of the 4-11 in the stockyards and that his buggy was on its way to pick him up. Joe Mackey arrived at 722 South Ashland Avenue Blvd. at Chief Horan's home, it is about a two mile distance from the firehouse. William Moore ran around the rear of the Chief's residence. Under a shelf was a secret buzzer that Moore pressed and Chief Horan answered "I will be right there". The chief's wife was also awakened by the buzzer and said, "What is it Jimmy?" The Chief answered, "Nothing, Dear, just another fire" as he left his home.

Before he got into the auto, the chief pulled a warm sweater over his head. It was 4:46 am. They drove as fast as the automobile would take them down Ashland Blvd to 41st Street. They turned left into the stockyards at 41st Street and then traveled East to Packers Avenue where they turned and traveled south. After Joe Mackey passed up 43rd Street, the Chief looked out his window and said, "The fire is one block west." He ordered Mackey to turn right on 44th Street and to then turn onto Loomis Street where he told him to park the auto.

It was 5:05 am when Chief Horan arrived at the scene. He put on his fire gear and started walking north on Loomis Street. It was still dark outside and there was a lot of smoke, but no fire could be seen.

Once Chief Horan arrived on the platform, he looked around at the boxcars and the canopy overhead and he made a face as Chief Burroughs met him. Chief Burroughs informed Horan that they just lost pressure in all lines. Chief Horan yelled at Burroughs, "Why don't we have the freight doors open?" He looked at Chief Lacey, and yelled "you have been here for over forty-five minutes. Why don't you have more hose lines on the fire? Get more hose lines in here right now" he yelled.

Chief Horan moved closer to the service door entrance, where the three lines were directing their streams through the freight doors that Truck 18 had opened. Chief Horan got down on his knees and crawled into the burning warehouse, Chief Lacey yelled, "Chief the building is weakening from the fire".

The Chief backed out onto the platform, again he yelled, "Get these freight doors open and let's get some water on this fire that is venting up the stairway to the left". Chief Lacey again tried to tell Chief Horan to back down. But, now Chief Horan got mad as hell, and ordered Chief Lacey to immediately bring in two more lines!

The smoke was choking the firemen, and Chief Horan ordered the firemen of Truck 18 to chop a hole in that canopy over their heads to vent the smoke out. Chief Lacey and the truckmen went north on the platform to a straight ladder that led up to the canopy. Chief Horan met Lieutenant Bradenburg of Truck 11, and ordered him to get those young guys of yours to chop open these freight doors. Chief Burroughs got close to Horan and informed him that the firemen tried to get in but there was just too much fire.

Chief Horan told Burroughs, "All the fire is to the left, I just saw it when I was in there. How many lines do we have working?" Chief Horan yelled!

Chief Burroughs yelled back, "We have five streams working and three engine companies waiting for water back on the platform by the boxcars". The large freight doors were finally opened, and engine streams began extinguishing the fire as they moved in little by little. The small band of brave firemen were in a hand- in-hand battle with this fire. Chief Burroughs told Chief Horan, "I think we better back down, Chief". Chief Horan just moved forward with Engine 59, as they struggled with their heavily charged fire hose line.

At 5:08 am, right in the midst of the battle, there was a strange stillness.

Some say they heard a moaning and cracking noise, and there was a yell up above from Joe Mackey who was on top of the canopy. The walls of the six-story brick building buckled outward about ten feet and instantly fell with an awful weight that shook the ground under the firemen's feet. The canopy that was above the firemen offered no more resistance than tissue paper would to the blow of a hammer!

The whole front of the structure collapsed, leaving the floors sagging, with meat and hog heads, all sliding down on top of the bricks. The wind offered oxygen and now the fire began to rage throughout the structure. Firemen out on Loomis Street just looked at the burning structure in shock as the catastrophe occurred before their startled and horrified eyes.

Without even given any consideration to their own safety, twenty to thirty firemen rushed up the pile of debris. Barrels of pickled meat were still sliding off the upper floors and onto the pile where the firemen caught under the collapse were buried. The assault on the main pile by the firemen was hopeless; the bricks and timber were so hot that it burned through their gloves!

Captain Alexander Lannon was pulled from the rubble on the north end of the platform; he was rushed to the hospital. The pile was so hot the firemen had tears in their eyes knowing they had to retreat as their brothers lay buried under tons of molten bricks and timbers! First Assistant Fire

Marshal Seyferlich, arrived on the scene. He was completely stunned by the sight of this catastrophe that lay before him. He knew that he too would have been inside that pile right next to Chief Horan. As he approached the burning mass, he was well aware of the tragedy that had just taken place.

Chief Seyferlich ordered the 1st special alarm at 5:12 am, to get more help immediately. The Fire Alarm Office sent five engine companies and three hook and ladders companies. After viewing the enormous task of uncovering all the debris that had toppled on top of the firemen, Chief Seyferlich requested a 2nd special alarm. The fire raged fiercely as the firemen regrouped, and more fire hoses were stretched down the Chicago Junction railroad tracks along Loomis Street.

More than twelve engine streams were now concentrating on the fire in the area of the collapse where the firemen were buried. At 5:20 am, Chief Seyferlich requested a 3rd special alarm. There were many injured firemen and it took more firemen to help them get them urgent medical attention. As the new arriving fire companies began making lead way, they drove the fire back into the building and extinguished most of it on the upper floors. But it was still unsafe to get to the pile of debris that covered the unknown number of firemen that were missing. The fire companies, who were fighting the initial fire, were crushed by the falling wall, and there were over forty firemen that were injured. There are others that were worn out by the heat of the fire, the cold of the winter; they were just exhausted beyond human endurance, but they continued their work bravely.

More bad news was reported to Chief Seyferlich at 6:50 am. The Battalion Chiefs informed him that the fire had now extended north into Warehouse 6, almost three hours after the still alarm. Chief Seyferlich requested a 4th special alarm, and the Englewood Fire Alarm Office dispatched another five engine companies.

After sizing up warehouse 6, the Chief again requested the 5th special alarm, bringing five more engines and three hook and ladders companies to the fire. At this time, all fire companies were working to full capacity and they now had seventeen streams working on the fire.

Again a small band of firemen crawled up the pile of bricks and timber over the top of the boxcars and began removing the still hot bricks. They began digging down to where their brother firemen were buried, but again were forced back by the raging fire and searing heat. Chief Seyferlich ordered the firemen to stay back until it could be cooled down.

At 7:47 am the weary Chief again requested the 6th special alarm and this time the Englewood Fire Alarm Office dispatched nine more engine companies. News came back to the scene that the Captain of Engine 50, Alexander Lannon, died in the hospital from his injuries.

At 7:59 am all 200 firemen coming on duty at 8:00 am were to report directly to the fire scene at 43rd and Loomis Street. The fresh firemen who began arriving at the scene began to give a much needed break to those who had been fighting this fire and manning the hoses for hours. In the next three hours the firemen in the area of the collapse had cooled down the bricks and burning timbers. By 11:30 am firemen started using an organized method to recover the pile of debris. They did this in an effort to uncover their buried brothers.

The work began on the north end of the pile were a helmet was found. It belonged to Chief William Burroughs, and shortly after finding that helmet, another helmet was found. The firemen knew they were in the right place. Then the first body was found, it was Captain Patrick Collins of Engine 59. Alongside of him was his pipeman, George Murawski of Engine 59.

Later, two more bodies were found right next to each other. Both of them were truckmen from Hook and Ladder 18, Charles Moore and Nicholas Crane. Their bodies were laid on stretchers and carefully lifted over the pile onto a boxcar then lowered down to Loomis Street where they were taken to an awaiting ambulance.

The fifth body to be found and removed from this debris pile was that of Second Assistant Fire Marshal William J. Burroughs. As his body was being slowly lowered down ladders that were set up to climb up onto the overturned boxcar; many hands went up to assist with lowering the stretcher down to Loomis Street. Respectfully, his face was covered with a rubber fire coat as he was carried down Loomis Street to an awaiting ambulance.

All of the work had stopped and the firemen of Chicago removed their helmets, and they briefly stood and watched as his body passed by them. All day long this scene was reenacted, and the next body that was found was that of William Weber, the driver of Engine Company 59, who had just moved into his new home three days before.

Heavy timbers and tons of bricks had been removed before the firemen found a crushed head and a torso that was smashed beyond recognition. The bodies lay side by side, and they were found with their arms over their faces, so as to protect themselves. Just before noon time a loud crack was heard and the upper half of the floors fell, pushing out the south wall of Warehouse 7. The work on the pile stopped but only for a short while and they then resumed the gruesome task once again.

The next body to be found and recovered was that of William Sturm of Engine 64, and the gruesome task of digging continued. Despite the cold winter weather with ice everywhere, the firemen crawled back into the pile and the digging became much more difficult now. Heavy timbers were found along with a mass of twisted iron pipes that ran under the canopy. The firemen found an unidentified body, and he did not have Chicago Fire Department fire gear on, but he was with them when the wall fell. The next body to be found was one of the watchmen and firemen for the Nelson-Morris company, His name was Andrew Dzurman. Very close to him was another body, Pipemen George Enthof of Engine Company 23.

The unidentified body that had been found earlier was a young boy named Steven Leen, a clerk for the Chicago Junction Railroad. The count of the dead was now at ten, Chief Steyferlich told the firemen to keep going until we recover each and every one of our firemen.

The dangerous work continued and the 11th body that was found and recovered was at 2:45 pm. It was pipeman, Thomas Costello, of Engine Company 29. A stretcher was brought in to what now looked like a pit. His body was covered with a rubber fire coat to hide the disfigurement caused by tons of brick and timbers that fell on him.

It wasn't fifteen minutes later, you could hear the voice of Chief Seyferlich calling for another stretcher. His voice was weak and you could hear the sorrow in his voice. The body was carefully lifted out of the ruins and placed on the stretcher and he was covered with a rubber fire coat. "Who is it" a fireman called out. "It is Nicolas Doyle, the son of Captain James Doyle," a voice called back. Truck man Nicolas Doyle of hook and ladder 11. His father is still among the missing. As the body was passed back, tears were streaking down the soot covered faces of the firemen.

The 13th body that was found and removed was that of truckman, Albert Moriatry, of hook and ladder 11

The fire had extended through the weakened walls of Warehouse 7 and into Warehouse 6. This was more trouble for the firemen; as if they didn't have enough.

The tactic for fighting the fire in Warehouse 6 was to close off all the entrances and not allow any oxygen into the structure. Firemen were sent up to the roof of Warehouse 6. It was a seven-story brick building with wooden floors and roof. Many small holes were chopped into the roof and in each hole a hose line was placed inside. The hose was weighed down and secured, and they were unmanned, because Chief Seyferlich said, "we were not going to lose another fireman because of a building".

Mayor Fred Busse and his department Commissioners watched from across Loomis Street. They were standing on the canopy that covered the platform of the Armour Packing House. Also standing on top of the Armour canopy were the most prominent names in the meat packing industry including Edward Morris and his sons. The fire continued to burn and a railroad wrecking company began removing a few of the refrigerated boxcars that were crushed by the fallen wall.

The boxcars were pulled away using heavy chains so the firemen could now dig from two sides of the pile. The 14th and 15th bodies that were found almost together were that of Lieutenant Herman Brandenberg, and the torso of Truckman Edward Schonsett. Today was Edward Schonsett's birthday. Both were members of Hook and Ladder Company 11. A short distance away was his head and arm. Found still in his right hand was his axe handle. Although the arm was severed he still kept the grasp on his axe, and they carried Edward Schonsett out with the axe in his hand.

Large arc lights were placed across Loomis Street on top of the Armour Meat Company canopy, but down in the pit, they needed hand held lanterns. As the darkness of night came upon the firemen, they just continued to dig. Another body that was found and removed was that of Lieutenant Edward Danis of Engine Company 61.

The fire burned inside of building 6, and finally vented through the roof. Again, there was the danger of another wall that could collapse. The firemen in the ruins were pulled out and were told to wait in the safe area. It was now 9:00 pm, 17 hours from the time of the initial still alarm. Many engine streams were concentrated on the two burning buildings and in a short time the fires were finally brought under control.

Chief Seyferlich again sent the exhausted firemen back into the ruins to resume their search. It wasn't long before they found the body of James Fitzgerald of Engine Company 23; he was to be married on Christmas Eve. Just a few minutes later, they found the body of Chief Horan, he was found in a sitting position with his arms folded across his chest, and with his head down. The Chief's helmet was still on his head, and that protected his face, but his skull was fractured which most likely caused his death immediately. A large heavy timber was lying on his leg that was nearly severed below the knee. After carefully chopping away the heavy beam, freeing the Chief's leg, the firemen placed him on a stretcher and carried his broken body out of the ruins of the Nelson-Morris & Company warehouse.

Chief Horan's body was carried along the railroad tracks on Loomis Street that were covered with many fire hoses leading into the fire. His body was placed into a waiting ambulance where it was transported to the funeral home of his brothers Daniel Horan located at 307 East 61st Street.

Back at the site, the work of recovering the bodies of the remaining firemen continued. Since they all were working closely with Chief Horan, the bodies of truckmen, Michael McInerary and Peter Powers both of Truck Company 11 and pipeman Frank Walter of Engine 59, were found next to each other. A special fireman for the Nelson-Morris & Company Patrick Reaph was also found in the debris, just a short time later.

The last body recovered was that of Captain Dennis Doyle, of Engine Company 39 he is the father of Nicolas Doyle of Truck 11 who was found earlier.

The fire in the two warehouses continued to burn throughout the day. While working at the scene, firemen found the shield and the eagle that was worn on Chief Horan's helmet, Chief Seyferlich ordered it to be taken to Chief Horan's office in City Hall.

As the news of the fatal fire filtered throughout the City the fallen firemen's widows lined up at McInerery's undertaking parlor, located at 600 West 43rd Street. All day long the broken bodies of the firemen were laid out in the morgue at the rear of the parlor. The wife of William Weber waited for a long time and she asked if she could see her husband. The police officer at the entrance door said, "No, you will be better off not seeing him in this condition."

As tears ran down her face, she exclaimed, "I don't care what he looks like. I want to see my husband!" Mrs. Brandenburg went to console her as the two weeping widows were escorted away by the Chicago Police. In the late evening, the scene was re-enacted over and over again as the families came to identify their husbands, brothers, and fathers.

The last body to be removed from the ruins was Captain Dennis Doyle of Engine 39. His body was transported to King's undertaking room to lay by that of his son, Nicholas Doyle, whose body the first was taken from the Nelson-Morris plant 7.

The bodies were being prepared for burial and an emergency meeting was held by Mayor Busse, where he appointed a Committee of fifteen Aldermen to make sure that all the burials were to go smoothly and with reverence. This committee was authorized to make any and all arrangements for the burial of these brave firemen. They were to prepare suitable and fitting memorials for all those who died.

One of the first funerals was that of Second Assistant Fire Marshall William J. Burroughs. He was laid to rest in Oakwood Cemetery.

Services for Pipeman George E. Enthof of Engine Company 23 was held at his residence and he was to be laid to rest at Wunder's Cemetery.

Services for William F. Weber would be at Sacred Heart Church, he was to be laid to rest at Mount Olivet Cemetery.

Captain Dennis N. Doyle of Engine 390 along with his son, Nicholas Doyle Truckman of Hook & Ladder 11 were laid to rest at Mount Olivet Cemetery.

Lieutenant William G. Sturm of Engine Company 64 was to have services at Masonic Temple and he was to be laid to rest in Mount Hope Cemetery.

Pipeman Frank W. Walters of Engine Company 59, was to be laid to at Calvrey Cemetery escorted by members of Engine 59.

Lieutenant Heerman G. Brandberg of Hook & Ladder 11, services were to be held at his residence and he was to rest at Oakwood Cemetery.

Lieutenant Edward Danis of Engine 61, services were held at his residence he was laid to rest at Oakwood Cemetery.

Services for Truckman Albert J. Moriarity of Hook & Ladder 11 were held St. Elizabeth Church, and he was laid to rest at Mount Olivet Cemetery.

Services for Truckman Nicholas Crane of Hook & Ladder 18 were at St. Gabriel's Church, he was laid to rest at Mount Olivet Cemetery.

Services for Truckman Charles Moore of Hook & Ladder 18 were at his residence, he was laid to rest at Mount Greenwood Cemetery on Christmas Day.

Services for Pipeman Thomas J. Costello of Engine Company 29 were held at St. David's Church, he was laid to rest at Mount Olivet Cemetery.

Services for Truckman Peter J. Powers of Hook & Ladder 11 were be at St. James Church, he was laid to rest at Mount Carmel Cemetery.

Services of the Chief of the Brigade James Horan Fire Marshal of the Chicago Fire Department were held at Holy Name Cathedral. A very impressive scene of thousands of mourners packed the cathedral. From the cathedral, a detail of fifty mounted Policeman escorted the body of the martyred Chief to Calvary Cemetery where he was laid to rest.

The long series of funerals of the victims of the stockyard fire continued for five days after the fire when the bodies of the twenty-four men killed by the fallen wall were laid to rest. Thousands of citizens watched the slow processions of the funerals. Chicago felt its bereavement and the news of the tragic deaths spread countrywide as almost every section of the city would see at least one cortege of a fallen fireman.

The Christmas of 1910 in Chicago had to be one of its darkest days. The grief and the mourning were felt through out the city. Flags of public schools throughout the city were lowed to half mast and were kept lowered in honor of the firemen killed in the union stockyards until they all were buried.

The big fire probe began with the Cook County Coroner, Peter Hoffman, who started the extensive investigation of the Morris & Company fire, which caused the deaths of twenty-four brave men. They jury that was impaneled by the coroner went to the scene of the fire at 10 am.

Hoffman said, "I hear that there was a lack of water pressure and if such is the case I shall learn whose duty it was to maintain the pressure and who neglected it". Coroner Hoffman continued, "I am going to ask the Building Department, the Fire Department, and the Electric Departments of this City to each delegate a representative to assist the jury in its investigation. What we are looking for is the condition of the walls, the weight capacity load of the floors, what each floor was used for, the wiring conditions and all other details that may be relevant to this disaster."

A fund was started, which was called: "Firemen's Relief Fund." The Tribune will receive subscriptions to the fund to be raised for the widows and orphans of the firemen killed in the stockyards fire The fund will be turned over to the duly appointed trustees.

The organization of the Citizens Committee, through the selections of more than seventy sub-committees, representing nearly all the lines of commercial and professional activity in the city, announced the central committee will manage all the money of the sub-committee. The central committee, of which Harlow N. Higinbotham is Chairman, also will meet to discuss ways and means to handle the contributions coming directly into its hands. Mr. Higinbatham and other members of the committee were absent from the city so no meeting was possible.

In respect to the dead, Chicago will watch the dawn of the New Year, without any of the shouting, horn blowing, or bell ringing that in previous yeas have created pandemonium in the loop district. It is the decree of Chief of Police Steward that any celebrations must be both orderly and respectful. There will be three to four policemen per block in the downtown loop, and any disorder will be suppressed immediately.

Questions are being asked, as to whose negligence made martyrs of these heroes. This is not the time to harshly prejudge City officials or private corporations that many have been responsible for events that led to deficient water pressure, poor electrical wiring or dangerous housing of explosive materials at the Morris Packing plant. This will come out at the official inquiry, and public sentiment will insist upon such inquiry being most thorough and searching. That is the reason that Coroner Peter Hoffman has taken steps to investigate each and every aspect of this incident.

It has been said, that no higher tribute can be paid to Chief Horan and his martyred firemen, than they perished bravely in the performance of their duty. Hundreds of times, these heroes have faced death, so that others might escape death. Yet the real lesson of this tragedy, as in other similar ones that have preceded it, is that fire preventive measures are the responsibility of all city administrators. Chief Horan tried to introduce building inspections into his newly established "Bureau of Combustibles", but he did not get that far.

There is little expectation of any criminal responsibility being fastened on any person or corporation, however, an analysis of the conditions and circumstances which conspired to cause the tragedy is certain to be carefully assessed, and censure will be administered where due.

Coroner Hoffman instructed Morris & Company to have present at the inquest, all persons familiar with the construction and use of the building. Members of the jury visited Morris and Company, and a set of written questions were left that needed to be answered at the inquest. All reports about fire alarm boxes and the distance between fire hydrants will also be scrutinized.

Witnesses to testify were all officers, and members of the first alarm fire companies who responded and Paul Leska, the night watchman, who discovered the fire. Each and every witness was heard and all reports were explained by the heads of their departments.

Listed below, from the Cook County Coroner's jury findings of from the stockyards fire on Thursday, December 22, 1910, are the fire conditions at the time of the collapse of the six-story brick wall:

The fire was burning in a confined space under conditions which generated large volumes of gases and generated products of combustion not wholly consumed, due to the lack of sufficient air supply. The opening of the large freight doors, allowed fresh air to reach the seat of the fire, in the above described conditions. Because of the fresh oxygen fueling the fire, the rate of combustion suddenly increased, so as to create a great pressure sufficient enough to cause the collapse of the east wall of the Morris Meat Plant 7.

There was mention of the explosion, but of all the witnesses, no one can say they heard an explosion. People are upset with the ruling of the Jury. There just is no criminal responsibility to allow anyone to point a finger at. Some say that Morris & Co. knew their wall to be unsafe. This fact was established. Yet, what did Morris & Company do to make these walls safe? Nothing! The stockyard company knew that the water pressure was below the point of safety. What did they do to remedy it? Nothing!

Nancy Doolan found the newspaper printed lists of those who contributed to the relief fund for the widows and orphans of these brave men. There has been a significant silence on the part of the beef barons who have not sent in a contribution to this Fund. Not one dollar will any of them give to the fund until they have been shamed into giving it and then they will give as little as they can to escape criticism. Nancy was told about the beef barons' unwillingness to help when she told the story about clothes she had for Mrs. Moore's three-year old. Mrs. Moore is a very bitter woman who is unable to cloth or feed her children.

"No one is at fault. Is there any negligence, somewhere?" Alice Moore said. "There are twenty four men who are dead and there isn't even a little negligence. Building inspections that still permit dangerous firetraps to exist is no more and no less criminal than a system of inspections that allows sub-standard careless wiring and the storing of dangerous explosive material, near these combustible structures."

These sale committees, which were sub-committees of the Citizens Central Committee, were created to solicit contributions to the fund. They started working in a city-wide canvas for what Harlow Higinbotham thinks could be a goal of collecting $250,000.

Checks and cash began to pour into the headquarters of the Citizens Central Committee of the Illinois Trust and Savings Bank. All the collections are being turned over to John Mitchell, the Treasurer for the Citizens Committee.

"In view of the fact that the World's Fair Fire had fourteen lost lives, and that $104,000 was raised I believe this new fund for the loss of twenty-four lives, should be able to collect well over $200,000," the Chairman said. Chairman Higinbotham said the experience gained from the World's Fair Fire Fund would be valuable, and I only hope that all separately collected funds will converge into our central fund so that its apportionment may be made and used to the greatest advantage possible.

Subscriptions were being made even outside of Chicago. Children brought in their piggy banks and gave it all to the children who just lost their fathers. The sub-committee worked very hard meeting with companies to try to raise the fund to at least $250,000 for the benefit of the widows and orphans. When the ten day campaign was over they were sure that they had raised the amount set by Chairman Harlow N. Higinbotham.

The cold winter months of January and February seemed to slip by. The city still mourns, but they begin to put the Chicago Fire Department back together again. Fires still occur and the firemen respond and extinguish the fires. When a loss that is so great sometimes the only thing to heal it is time and going back to work. Mayor Busse could not replace Chief James Horan yet, so he appointed Chief Seyferlich and as the acting Chief Fire Marshal in charge of the Chicago Fire Department.

It was found out by a few firemen that Mrs. Moriarity, the wife of Al Moriarity on of Truck 11, who was killed in the stockyards, had to move from her home because she couldn't pay the rent. Norm was over at Engine 50's firehouse when he found out that Mrs. Moriarity had moved back in with her mother.

The firemen of Engine 50 said, "Hey how about the fund for the widows and orphans, isn't that suppose to help". Nancy pulled out the list of the widows and where they lived and she said that started asking questions of the widows about assistance they were receiving from the fund.

None of them had any assistance from the fund or anywhere else. Four of the widows had to give up their homes; Mrs. Moriarity Mrs. Doyle, Mrs. Costello and Mrs. Moore are living in with relatives, because they can't afford to live alone with their children.

"Nancy," I said, "These women need to meet, all of them, at one location, and soon". Nancy went to see Mrs. Moriarity, who seemed to be the kind who could lead these women. Alice Moriarity said, "All I have received from anyone was eighty-six dollars in three months since the death of my husband." The last check from the city was nine days short, because Al didn't quite work a full month.

"I would like to see Mr. Higinbotham try to live three months on eight-six dollars like we have done," said Mrs. Moriarity. "I get thirty-five dollars a month and my son gets eight dollars a month until he is sixteen years old. I have read in the newspapers that almost a quarter of a million dollars has been subscribed for our benefit, but we have never seen as much as one dollar of the fund."

Nancy Doolan helped Mrs. Moriartity with an invitation to her home for the discussion of the fund. Each invitation was hand delivered by special firemen and only to the nineteen widows who were invited.

The next evening eighteen women, clothed in deep black, seventeen widows of firemen, and one mother of a dead fireman met at the home of Mrs. John Lannon, 5735 South Emerald Avenue. Transportation door to door was provided by some special firemen. These women passed a resolution at this meeting demanding to know what has become of the fund collected by public subscription. They passed resolutions demanding an accounting of the fund, and also wanted to be given representation on the committee that is handling the money.

A permanent organization to be known as The Sockyards Fire Survivors Protective Association was formed by the women. The resolutions unanimously were passed and a copy of resolutions was sent to Harlow Niles Higinbotham, Chairman of the Citizens Committee.

Three of the widows called on Mayor Busse and asked him about the fund. The Mayor said that he was a member of the Committee and he thinks that there has been one meeting about the fund, but he was not sure. Mayor Busse said he does not have any information on the distribution of the funds but he promised he would get a meeting together for the widows with Harlow Higinbotham. Something must have come up because the widows never heard from Mayor Busse.

The plan of the widows was to have the fund of $211,000 administered so that the children would each receive interest on $2,000 until they are 21 years of age, and then they are to receive the principal. After the money for the children is subtracted from the fund, the remainder is to be divided among the surviving widows without regard to the rank held by the fireman that were killed.

They have had the money in their passion for some months. Most of the widows designated by the givers as beneficiaries, are dissatisfied with the arrangements made by this committee. The widows say that the money was given for them, it belongs to them, and they want their respective shares of it now! But, the Citizens Committee of Higinbotham, Sunny, Mitchell, Wilson, were to be utterly adverse to giving these widows their money, and resolved to hold on to it until such time as it shall please them to give the widows so much of it as they see fit! So the widows would have to take them into court to get their money.

The law suit was filed just yesterday, Monday, April 17, 1911, by counsel representing the widows, Mr. John Coburn, who will not take any money from the widows for his services. John Coburn called for the immediate relief for the widows who are basically starving and losing their homes.

The Citizens Committee and Chairman Harlow Higinbotham have taken the $211,000 and they have invested this money in trusts by buying stocks, bonds, and securities. The members of this committee invested all the funds in bonds. The income will be paid to the beneficiaries, while the principal will be retained as a permanent endowment fund.

The money or a large part of it has been invested in the Chicago Edison Company, The Chicago Railway Company, and The Chicago Telephone Company. Why were those bonds chosen as proper investments for the money which rightfully belongs to the widows and orphans? Because it is known that Mr. Higinbotham and several others on the committee are very heavy stockholders in these three companies, which return them dividends.

The $211,000 is being handled by Mr. John Mitchell, who is the President of Illinois Trust and Savings Bank and it is very likely that the bonds and money are still being held by the bank for a service fee of course of one thousand dollars per year. This is not the first time that this same group of businessmen were involved with firemen. Some years ago there was a fire at the World's Fair in 1893. The fire was in a cold storage building on the grounds of the fair and fifteen men were killed; 12 of them were Chicago Firemen. These same charitable gentlemen acquired control of a fund of $104,000 in the same manner, as they did here with the stockyards fire fund. There are some thousands of dollars of that fund unaccounted for and no one seems to know just where it is.

Mr. Sunny and Harlow Higinbotham were both Directors of the Cold Storage Fire Fund in 1893. When they were asked about that fund, Mr. Sunny said that there was twenty- nine thousand dollars left in the fund. Mr. Higinbotham said there was eleven thousand left in the fund and the person at the Illinois Trust and Savings Bank, where the money was deposited, told us that there was nothing left in that account; that is was all paid out in claims. But, to whom were the payouts made to?

The Citizens of Chicago raised a fund of $211,000 for the relief of the widows and children whose fathers and husbands lost their lives in the stock yards fire four months ago. Not one penny of the fund has been turned over to these struggling widows and children. Mr. Coburn, for the widows said that he characterized the members of the relief committee as a bunch of alleged charitable gentlemen who made it their business to grab control of every relief fund raised by the fund. The Committee stated that money was needed for immediate relief of the suffering widows and orphans. As far as can be learned, not one of the widows has yet received any relief, immediate or otherwise.

Harlow Higinbotham had an important part in the control of the Cold Storage Fire Relief Fund. The widows and beneficiaries of that fund appealed for a division of that money, but Higinbotham and his associates refused to grant their request. Mr. Coburn asked, "Has anyone seen a report from Harlow N. Higinbotham regarding that money during the last ten years? We hope to get answers to those questions as well as others affecting the stockyards fire fund when the hearing continues tomorrow."

Higinbotham again skillfully obtained control of $211,000 contributed for the widows and orphans of the men who died at the stockyards fire. He has refused to give them any of that money. He has emphatically declared himself against any proposition for a cash division of the money to the widows and orphans

The St. Leo Council, of the Knights of Columbus, whose 500 members contributed $500.00 to the stock yards fire fund have started an investigation of the committee action of this fund.

Mr. Higinbotham will have to answer several questions of this committee and top of that list are:

1. Why hasn't Mr. Higinbotham given out a statement to the public to explain exactly what has been done with the money that the people of Chicago donated to these women?
2. We want to know why the money has been invested in bonds so soon in the companies you are very interested in?
3. We want to know why Mr. Higinbotham has said to the Citizens Committee, we've decided to invest the money that thousands of people gave?
4. We know that $9,553 has been deducted from the widow's

fund as expenses for investing the money. You have taken that money from a fund without any explanation to anyone.

Word got out to the firehouses that Harlow Higinbotham and his hand- picked committee refused to give the widows any of the money that was donated to them by all of us.

There is a meeting of special firemen called over at Engine 61's firehouse. There will only be a chosen few who will be in the crew. The meeting took place and over 50 firemen showed up. The leader was Tom Collins from Truck 18, he told the firemen that we are going to find out why the money hasn't been given to the widows and we are going to silently talk to Higinbotham, Sunny, Mitchell, Wilson and Uptan, "I will cut his God dammed throat," someone yelled, "Shhh, if it comes to that, I will talk to you."

The firemen were broken into three firemen teams; we need to find out where they live and we will meet back here tomorrow night.

The first house that this squad of special firemen went to was Mr. Sunny's. They knew the time that he would get home so two guys followed him and once he got out of his automobile he was grabbed from behind and flipped into the wagon by two of the boys. They took him for a little ride to the lake for some questions!

They asked him why the widows did not receive any money. He was shaking in his boots. Sunny answered, "They were never going to get the money only the interest."

"Whose idea was this?" they asked him. "Higinbotham is the mastermind," Sunny said. "He put the word on the street about the grieving widows, took control of the money, and invested it in companies that he would profit from." "Where is Higinbotham?" the firemen asked. "I don't know; I haven't seen him in weeks," said Sunny.

"You know that you are going to court next week, Mr. Sunny, and I better hear those same words from you, or else; you see that big blue lake out there? You might be swimming in it, or floating in it." They left him there.

They were unable to find Higinbotham anywhere, but they found his daughter, Mrs. Rita Crane. She was taken into an alley in the loop by the boys. "We have a present for you, give it to your father." and they handed her a shoe box. They told her that he better release the money that was given to the widows and not to him as they left her.

Mr. Hutchins informed Mr. Sunny that he would not be paid out of the widow's money for his services. Higinbotham wasted no time and Mr. Sunny hired an ex judge, John Barton Payne who was assisted by John Wilson.

Mr. Hutchins knew the widows should have seen the money and he handed Mr. Mitchell back the check that was given to him. Both Payne and Wilson are high priced lawyers, and as they walked into the court room all knew that they were there to stop the widows from obtaining the fund. Harlow Niles Higinbotham was not in the courtroom, because his life had been threatened.

The shoebox that the boys gave to Higinbotham's daughter had a note saying in a box that read; You will be dead on May 5th Included in the box was dagger, and the box was lined with black velvet.

Mr. Coburn for the widows said in the court room, "Where is the committee? They sent their lawyers. Why? because they can't face the eighteen widows who have sat through all of this court room drama and have not received one dime. Mr. Higinbotham wants the money in his control. He can use it very effectively to suite his own purposes. He is determined to keep it and we are equally determined not to permit him to do so", said Coburn.

Mr. Coburn referred to a remark of the defense attorney for the committee that these women might marry again. So let them marry again, that is none of your business what these women do with their lives. The close of the case was marked by bitter clashes between attorneys for both sides and charges of unfairness were freely made. While the court case was going on, Mr. Harlow N. Higinbotham was on the train bound for New York City, because the "dagger" that was delivered to him made him a believer that his life was being threatened.

The information about Higinbotham returning to Chicago was not ascertained, no one knew one way or the other if he would ever return. It is thought that he would wait until all of the distribution of the fund was decided by the courts. Judge Cooper, before whom the matter is pending, had announced that he would not give his decision in the case until he returns from his vacation in September.

So the summer months passed, in which the widows and the children still had no assistance; June, July, and August, three months of waiting to hear the decision of Judge Cooper. It has been almost ten months since the fatal fire in the stockyards, and was supposed to get easier, but had not. It still hurts the widows deeply to think about their husbands

Mayor Busse finally made Chief Charles Seyferlich Chief Fire Marshal of the Brigade and the Fire Department began returning to some type of normalcy. Chief Seyferlich or "Big Sey" as he was called, was extremely popular with the firemen.

When the stockyards fire took the lives of so many firemen including his best friend Chief Jim Horan, "Big Sey" took control of that fire, and only took a short break to inform the Mayor of the progress, and then returned to the ruins to be with his men. As Fire Marshal he responded to every 2-11 alarm fire in the city to ensure the safety of his men. If one word could be used to sum up Chief Seyferlich, it was safety.

The day has come to find out the judge's decision. The court room was full, but the first row of seats was empty. The attorney, Mr. Coburn, for the widows put them in the comfortable place until everyone was in the court room. Eighteen widows and one mother of firemen who were killed in the stockyards fire entered into the court. The women were all dressed in black with long flowing veils of mourning.

Judge William Fenimore Cooper entered the courtroom and the bailiff yells out, "All rise." Judge Cooper pointed out that there were two controversies for him to decide over.

First, the distribution of the fund, as allotted to each beneficiary or branch of beneficiaries, a right and equitable one.

Second, does have the committee the right to tie up this fund in trust, without the express authority from the donors of the fund, or to pay the beneficiaries the interest income from the fund only, and not the fund itself.

In deciding the first point in favor of the committee Judge Cooper said, "Any plan of distribution could have been or could be adopted in this case would be open and subject of the objections stating apparent inequality. Take the whole sum and divide equally to the branches. Some of the dependents proportionally would be allowed more or less than others because the inequality of the number of persons in several branches. There is a vast difference between collecting money for a beneficiary and giving it to her in a lump sum. She may immediately use it to begin a new life for herself and her children. On the other hand, giving her only the income of it while the principal is withheld from her forever, eventually go to some person who maybe is yet unborn, and of whom the committee and donors never thought of

So here reads the law by Judge William Fenimore Cooper:

It is the law that where a fund is entrusted to an agent, trustee or other intermediary to be given to a third person, that the giving of this income or earnings, only of the fund, is not a satisfaction of the gift.

The court favors in the name of the widows and children and orders that $211,000 be distributed to the named beneficiary within the committee's apportionments as follows.

James Horan, Fire Chief:

Mrs. Margaret Horan, Widow	$17,000
Margaret Horan, Daughter	$5,000
William Horan, Son	$5,000
Ellen Horan, Daughter	$5,000
James Horan, Jr., Son	$5,000

William Burroughs, Second Assistant Fire Chief:

Mrs. Belle F. Burroughs, Widow	$11,586
Helen M. Burroughs, Daughter	$2,000

Patrick E. Collins, Captain:
Mrs. Alice Collins, Widow $5,253
Three children (each 2,000) $6,000

D.N. Doyle, Captain:
Mrs. Elizabeth Doyle, Widow $5,253

Alexander Lannon, Captain:
Mrs. Charlotte Lannon, Widow $5,253
Four children (each 2,000) $8,000

H.G. Brandenburg, Lieutenant:
Mrs. Helen Brandenburg, Widow $4,826

E.S. Davis, Lieutenant:
Mrs. Mary Davis, Widow $4,826
Three children (each 2,000) $6,000

W.G. Sturm, Lieutenant:
Mrs. Bertha Sturm,Widow $4,826
One child $2,000

T.J. Costello, Pipeman:
Mrs. Mary Costello, Widow $3,603
One child $2,000

Nicholas Crane, Truckman:
Mrs. Agnes Crane, Widow $3,605

Nicholas Dennis Doyle, Truckman
Mrs. Hannora Doyle, Widow $3,605
Two children $4,000

M.F. McInerny, Truckman:
Mrs. Mary McInerny, Widow $3,605
Three children $6,000

Charles N. Moore, Truckman:
Mrs. Elizabeth Moore, Widow $3,605
One child $2,000

H.J. Moriarity, Truckman:
Mrs. Mary Moriarity, Widow $3,605
One child $2,000

G.F. Murawski, Pipeman:
Mrs. Martha Murawski, Widow $3,605
Five children $10,000

P.J. Powers, Truckman:
Mrs. Alice Powers, Widow $3,605
One child $2,000

Edward D. Schonsett, Truckman:
Mrs. Minnie Schonsett, Widow $3,605
One child $2,000

F.H. Walters, Pipeman:
Mrs. Jennie Watlers, Widow $3,605

W.F. Weber, Driver:
Mrs. Margaret Weber, Widow $3,605
Three children $6,000

James J. Fitzgerald, Lieutenant (Unmarried):
Johanna Fitzgerald, Dependant Mother $2,000

George C. Enthof, Pipeman (unmarried):
Dependent Father and Mother $2,000

With the signing of a release by the widows of the fireman who lost their lives in the big stockyards fire last December, the long struggle between Harlow Niles Higinbotham and the widows was over. The widows all met at John Coburn's office in the loop, and their checks were handed to each one by attorney Coburn.

Attorney John Coburn planned to give a luncheon at the Boston Oyster house for the nineteen widows and one mother. A grand time was had. There was some cheering, some stories told and there was a lot of crying to each other.

An announcement was made with regard to Mr. Higinbotham; he was last seen on the dock in New York City. He called a press conference to tell his side of the story. The conference was at the gangway leading up to the White Star Ocean Liner Olympic. He told reporters he only wanted good for the widows and children. The fund was set up as an endowment not to be just given out

In the rear, one of the reporters, asked about the other funds that he created; the Cold Storage Fire, and the monument Higinbotham was going to build for the slain Mayor Carter Harrison "Where is that money, Mr. Higinbotham?" the reporter asked.

With that, Higinbotham went up the gangway and on to the ship. Once on top, he waited for all reporters to leave and then briskly walked down the gangway of the White Star Olympic, across the pier and boarded the ship "Mauretania" that his daughter is on. They were well out to sea when Mr. Higinbotham came up on deck to meet his daughter as they sailed to England.

At the luncheon the widows raised their glasses and said "May they never be forgotten".

THE END

THE HEROES OF THE STOCKYARD FIRE

James Horan
Fire Marshal and Chief of Brigade 1906-1910

PUBLISHED BY

H. E. DAVEY and H. W. HIGGINS
863 Dearborn Avenue
CHICAGO, ILL.

THE HEROES OF THE STOCKYARD FIRE.

Words & Music by
HENRY E. DAVEY.

We boast of the he-roes that fell in the bat-tles, We
The scene of the fire____ was one of great gran-deur; A

waged a-gainst In-di-ans Eng-land and Spain; Yet, strange as it seems, there is
sight, awe in-spir-ing; a sight ne'er for-got; But not a-mong Hor-an's brave

sel-dom a whis-per Of praise for the boys who died fight-ing the flame. The
squad was a cow-ard, And each went to du-ty and shared the same lot. The

158

4

stock - yards were burn - ing, the fire - men re - spond - ed With
boys, near - ly smoth - ered, and blind - ed, and wound - ed, Stuck

gal - lop - ing hors - es and clang of the bell; And
no - bly to du - ty un - til a wild yell Of

on - to their du - ty of sav - ing the ci - ty, They
warn - ing rang out; but 'twas too late to save them; The

tore a - way fear - less - ly and no - bly fell.
walls top - pled o - ver; be - neath them they fell.

Stockyard Fire - 3

CHORUS. (Lively)

Three cheers for those he-roes that fell in their ef-fort To save hu-man life at the cost of their own; No time shall e-rase from our mem-'ry their brav-'ry; Their deed is re-cord-ed in hist-'ry and poem. Three hist-'ry and poem.

Stockyard Fire - 3

The Chicago Firefighters' Monument was erected at the entrance gate to Chicago's Stockyards where the twenty-one firefighters honored in this book ,gave their lives in a fire on December 22, 1910. The monument was built to honor all Chicago Firemen who died in the line of duty,
Christopher Wheatly's, who died August 9, 2010, will have his name engraved on the monument on October 8, 2010
The Monument Committee
Bil Cantorini
Bill Cosgrove
Bill Przbylski

A Prayer for Firemen

When they are called to duty, God
Whenever flames may rage
Give them the strength to save some life,
Whatever be its age,
Help them embrace a little child before it is too
late,
Or save an older person
From the horror of that fate
Enable them to be alert
And hear the weakest shout
And quickly and efficiently
To put the fire out
And if according to Your will
They have to lose their lives
Please bless with Your hand
Their children and their wives.

Made in the USA
Middletown, DE
11 August 2015